# The Psychology of Religious Knowing

Fraser Watts
and
Mark Williams

GEOFFREY
CHAPMAN

**Geoffrey Chapman**
A Cassell imprint
Villiers House, 41/47 Strand, London WC2N 5JE
387 Park Avenue South, New York, NY 10016-8810

First published 1988 by Cambridge University Press
First published in paperback 1994

*British Library Cataloguing-in-Publication Data*

Watts, Fraser N.
The psychology of religious knowing.
1. Psychology, Religious   2. Experience (Religion)
1. Title     II. Williams, Mark
200′.1′9   BL53

*Library of Congress Cataloging-in-Publication Data*

Watts, Fraser N.
The psychology of religious knowing / Fraser Watts and Mark
Williams.
p.  cm.
Originally published: Cambridge; New York: Cambridge University
Press, 1988.
Includes bibliographical references and index.
1. Experience (Religion)   2. Knowledge, Theory of (Religion)
3. Psychology, Religious.   I. Williams, J. Mark G.   II. Title.
[BL53.W33  1994]
291.4′2 – dc20                                        94–22340
                                                        CIP

ISBN 0–225–66760–6

Cover picture: Ezekiel's Vision, reproduced from Nicholas of Lyra's
*Postillae* on the Old Testament, presented to St Alban's Abbey in 1457
and now in the Cambridge University Library. By permission of the Syndics
of the Cambridge University Library.

Printed and bound in Great Britain by Biddles Ltd, Guildford and King's Lynn

# Contents

*To our parents*
*Norman and Audrey Watts*
*John Howard and Barbara Williams*

# Acknowledgements

This book has been a long time germinating, and we each feel indebted to the many people who have helped to bring us to the point of being able to write it. Much of the preparation occurred while we were developing separately our approaches to the issues concerned, and before we made the decision to write the book together. Many of the people to whom we feel most indebted have had no part in the actual writing of the book; indeed some do not even know of its existence. Clearly, then, they can in no way be held responsible for the use we have made of their ideas.

One of Fraser's earlier debts is to Bishop Stephen Verney. 'He helped me to understand the richness of the Christian contemplative tradition, and especially the way it has developed in the East. The late John Davy, former science editor of *The Observer* and Vice-Principal of Emerson College, helped me to see the potential of imaginative cognition and to understand its scientific and spiritual significance. Owen Barfield, though scarcely even an acquaintance, showed me through his books what metaphor can be. Chapter 9 is largely a development and application of his ideas. The influence of John Davy and Owen Barfield came together with developments in experimental psychology that led to a kind of 'conversion' to *cognitive* psychology. I remember vividly the intellectual excitement of the winter of 1974–5 as I saw something of the importance and potential scope of an emancipated and rigorous approach to human cognition. There followed an early attempt to set out some of the ideas of this book in a series of articles in *Theoria to Theory*, a Journal edited by members of the Epiphany Philosophers. (We are grateful to the publishers, Gordon and Breach, for permission to re-work some of material from volumes 12 (1978) and 13 (1979) of *Theoria to Theory*, mostly in chapters 5 and 6 of the present book). In the course of preparing those articles, Dorothy Emmet and Jonathan Westphall, the editors, and the late Margaret Masterman, acting President of the Epiphany Philosophers, made many helpful suggestions that shaped the development of my ideas. I am particularly grateful to Jonathan, who originally suggested that I write the series, and who made his technical expertise in philosophy available to help us with chapter 4. More recently, Eric Hutchison, psychotherapist, scholar and priest, has helped me to understand better the inter-relationship of experience and doctrine, and to appreciate the contribution of Jung. Gerard Loughlin, David Healy and Brother Alistair, SSF, have read parts of the manuscript and made many helpful suggestions. I am especially grateful to Brother Alistair for his encouragement and enthusiasm, and for the openness with which, on numerous occasions, we have been able to share our attempts to follow the personal, intellectual and religious path of which this book is one manifestation.

Mark also owes a great debt to many people. 'Tom Moffatt first introduced me to the way philosophy and religion could illuminate each other. The late Professor George Caird, who was Principal of Mansfield College, Oxford, at the time I was in Oxford was a great source of inspiration not only through his preaching and writing, but in the warmth of his friendship. Charles Brock, Fellow at Mansfield and minister at Wheatley United Reformed Church, was also influential in developing a sense of the way psychology and religion could interact. Oxford also gave me the opportunity of getting to know Michael Argyle and Arthur Peacocke, both of whom, working in very different areas, have shown me that the scientific study of religion is possible and desirable. Since moving via Newcastle to Cambridge, I have shared much and learned much from Tony Leighton, Allan Jenkins, John Kemp, David Deeks, James Dickie, Nigel Hancock and Raymond Tomkinson. I am particularly grateful to Allan Jenkins for his willingness to read and comment upon parts of the text. Finally, I owe a tremendous debt to my own family. Firstly, to my nephew David and nieces Rebecca and Katie for occupying my own children, so that many discussions with their parents could take place and many ideas tested. Secondly, and most importantly, to my wife Phyllis and to Anne-Marie, Jennifer and Robert for the gentle way they have brought me down to earth.'

Writing a book such as this that spans several disciplines, and goes beyond our own subject of psychology, is necessarily a hazardous undertaking. We hope readers will feel we have been right to make the attempt and will forgive any inaccuracies that have crept in. The intellectual challenges facing religion in the late twentieth century are such as to make it necessary for people to take the risk of venturing outside their normal academic frontiers.

Fraser Watts

St Dunstan's day, May 1987

Mark Williams

# 1

# Introduction

Psychological investigations of religion have proved a difficult undertaking. Part of the problem is that psychologists have often rushed for explanations of religion before they have quite understood what they were seeking to explain. They have also too often studied the externals of religion rather than its heart. An awareness of these potential pitfalls has guided our own approach, and they will bear some development.

Psychologists have too often attempted a kind of reductionist explanation that would explain religion *away* in psychological terms. The dangers of reductionist explanations arise in many areas of psychology. Take heart disease as an example. We now know a good deal about the kind of personality characteristics and social stresses that increase the risk of heart disease. We also understand how people react emotionally to having a heart attack, and the kind of psychological resources needed to make a good recovery. Some people find this kind of psychological approach to illness objectionable because it may seem to imply that heart disease is exclusively a psychological phenomenon (i.e. that it can be 'reduced' to the psychological level). Of course, this is not at all what is being suggested. There is no intention to deny that other non-psychological factors are also relevant to heart disease.

Equally, when a psychological approach is taken to religious phenomena it is not being suggested that they can be understood wholly in these terms. Most human phenomena have many different facets, can be described from many different points of view, and are the result of many different causal factors. For it to be legitimate to take a psychological approach to heart disease or to religion it need only be conceded that they have a psychological aspect. There is no suggestion that an exhaustive account of religion can be given in psychological terms.

Psychologists have often chosen to study the externals of religion for the pragmatic reason that they are easily and objectively measured. The aspects of religion that are most easily measured are observable

1

phenomena like claiming to believe in God and going to Church. Obviously, these may reflect a deep religious commitment, but they do not necessarily do so. The challenge to psychologists is to find ways of understanding better what committed religious people would see as the inner core of religious experience and understanding. However, there are several obstacles to doing this. One obvious one is that religious experience, like all experience, is difficult to study in a systematic, reliable way. Another is that because religious experience is rather unpredictable, it may prove elusive when you try to study it.

What we present in this book is not an empirical study of religious experience. Rather, we have drawn on religious writings and on our own intuitions about what are the essential features of the religious mind. What we have attempted is an exercise in conceptual 'mapping', drawing out how the accounts of the religious mind offered by religious people map on to the concepts and theories that psychologists use to describe and understand experience generally. To psychologists who might have preferred a more empirical approach, we would point to the dangers of rushing to investigate something before you have understood what you are trying to study. In many branches of psychology, not just the psychology of religion, there is too much premature and under-conceptualised research.

We have written this book at least as much for a religious as for a psychological readership. Some religious people will see no need to relate religion to psychology at all. Even if they take our point that we are not attempting to offer reductionists explanations of religion, an integration of religion and psychology may seem pointless. We do not think this is a tenable position. Religious experience is in one sense such an inherently psychological phenomenon that religious writers over the centuries have necessarily used at least some kind of lay psychology in talking about it. One cannot, for example, talk about the experience of trying to pray without describing what are, from one point of view, psychological phenomena. Excising psychological concepts from religion is not an available option. The only alternative to attempting to use relevant concepts from contemporary psychology is to continue to use the somewhat opaque and dated psychological concepts which are traditionally used in talking about spiritual phenomena. Such language may have acquired specifically religious connotations, but to anyone interested in clear and effective communication it is not an attractive language. We suggest that those who seek to describe the religious life and to teach it need a clearer and more sharply focused language to describe the psychological component of the religious life, and we hope that we can make a contribution to the development of such a language.

There is another objection to our enterprise with which we have more sympathy. This is that the religious life is essentially a mystery, and that in its very nature it can never be made completely clear and intelligible. However, our readers should note that we are not suggesting that *all* aspects of the religious life can be mapped on to psychological concepts, only that some aspects of it can. Even though there are probably limits to the exercise of conceptual mapping that we have attempted, such mapping should, within these limits, draw on the clearest psychological concepts available.

We have not attempted to relate the whole of the religious mind to psychological theory, but have focused on one particular domain of religious experience and one corresponding area of contemporary psychology. To be specific we have sought to relate religious knowing to cognitive psychology. There were both religious and psychological considerations that converged to suggest this choice.

We will explain the religious reasons first. One of the core features of the religious life is coming to *know* from direct experience what may previously have been a mere matter of religious teaching or of faith. This does not necessarily produce any changes in *what* is known, though it may do so, but it changes very radically *how* it is known. Religious knowledge acquired through direct experience seems able to direct people's lives in a way that mere assent to doctrine does not. If one is interested in the inner core of religion, there are few more important things to understand than such direct religious knowing.

It is not only psychologists studying religion who are open to criticism on this count. Christian leaders, outside the evangelical or charismatic traditions, have also sometimes been cautious about appearing to attach too much importance to personal knowledge and experience. Whatever the reasons for this caution, it has resulted in many people assuming that the Christian churches have little serious interest in helping people to follow a path of personal religious transformation, and that for this it is necessary to turn to Oriental traditions. There are many who have turned to transcendental meditation on the assumption that nothing similar was available in Christianity. Without wishing to decry the meditative traditions of other religions, we are disappointed that Christianity has kept its own contemplative tradition so hidden that most 'outsiders', and perhaps quite a few 'insiders' are wholly unaware of it. There is a clear need, from the religious point of view, to find a more accessible way of talking more openly about the experiential path to religious understanding.

Reticence about personal religious knowledge has sometimes been buttressed by intellectual arguments, and some of these will be discussed in chapter 4. Some religious thinkers have rejected the idea of religious knowledge in favour of 'faith'. At the extreme there have been those who, following Pascal, have seen human knowledge as essentially corrupt and therefore inherently inappropriate to the apprehension of God. There have also been many philosophers who have argued that it is a mistake to imagine that religious belief can properly be called 'knowledge' of any kind. We will reject such arguments, and of course we are not the first to do so.

The 'cognitive' approach to religious knowing that we espouse goes neither to the extreme of regarding religious belief as not being based on observation nor to the opposite extreme of regarding it as following demonstrably from observation. This middle way is close to that which has developed recently in psychoanalytic work on religion. Though Freud's original position was to regard religion as a matter of mere wish-fulfilment and illusion, recent psychoanalytic theorising has suggested that it is to be located in an intermediate sphere that is one neither of private fantasy nor of external reality. Psychoanalytic approaches to religion today are less reductionist than they used to be.

We need to make absolutely clear here that we are not, as psychologists, commenting on whether or not religious beliefs are correct, whether they are justified by rational argument and empirical evidence. Our concern is rather with *how* people arrive at what they take to be religious knowledge. From this point of view, it is unnecessary to adjudicate on the correctness of presumed knowledge. It needs to be recognised that in everyday life all of us are mistaken about many things. Not everything can be investigated exhaustively. We often have to act on intuitions, on judgements based on inadequate data. When travelling in an unfamiliar foreign country, for example, we have to make many informed guesses about the significance of the conduct of those around us. Some of our conclusions will be correct; others will not. The point we want to emphasise here is that the processes by which we reach these conclusions are essentially similar, whether or not they are true. We can consider the psychological processes by which people reach presumed knowledge about religious matters without necessarily making any assumption about whether or not that presumed knowledge is justified or correct. It seems most likely that, in religion as in other things, people are sometimes right and sometimes wrong. The search for religious knowledge is probably of uncertain outcome; but it is not wholly without foundation. Our argument is not that religious knowledge is or is not rationally justified, only that it is 'cognitive' in the sense that it is reached by cognitive processes that are somewhat similar to those by which other forms of human knowledge are reached.

The psychological reason for being interested in the link between religious knowing and the psychology of 'cognition' is based chiefly on the astonishing growth of cognitive psychology over the last 20 years. In some ways it is a surprising development in view of the 'behaviourist' phase through which psychology passed earlier in the century, in which it was imagined that all that psychology could study objectively was external, observable behaviour. Compared to this limited perspective, the development of dependable methods for the scientific study of man as a 'knower' has come as a major advance. Memory, language, reasoning and consciousness are now back at the core of experimental psychology. Presently, there is a strong interest in building on these core concerns of cognitive psychology to increase our understanding of a wide range of everyday human phenomena. Approaches to the understanding of emotion and emotional disorders are one of the most prominent of current efforts to extend the scope of cognitive psychology. It is in a similar spirit that we have begun here to address religious knowing from the perspective of cognitive psychology. The closer to ordinary life cognitive psychology gets, the more relevant it becomes to this enterprise. We judge that the time is now right to begin to apply cognitive psychology to the understanding of religious knowing. As far as we are aware, this is one of the first books on the psychology of religion to reflect the cognitive revolution that has taken place in psychology.

Though we believe that cognitive psychology provides a useful map for the understanding of religious knowing, we are clear that it is with an unusual kind of knowing that we are concerned, though not necessarily a unique one. In chapter 5 we will examine some other cognitive processes that afford a reasonably close analogue of religious cognition. There is clearly something rather 'uncertain' about religious knowing. Not everyone develops a capacity for it, and even for those who do so, the capacity sometimes fades. In this it seems rather like aesthetic perception. Learning to 'see' a work of art is a similarly uncertain affair. Also, like religious knowing it demands both a certain detachment from distracting preoccupations and a degree of emotional involvement. Both of these contribute to the heightened attentiveness that seems to characterise both religious and aesthetic knowing. Sensitivity to other people, especially the capacity known as 'empathy' is another similar form of knowing.

However, probably the best analogue of religious knowing is the development of personal insight. How people gradually come to understand more about themselves seems in many ways to be similar to how they come to understand more about the things of God. Personal insights can develop in a great variety of circumstances, but psychotherapy constitutes a framework specifically designed to foster their development, and is therefore a convenient arena in which to study the psychological processes by which personal insights arise. Throughout this book, we will draw on this analogy between personal knowing and religious knowing.

Another helpful way of studying religious knowing is to look at the effects of meditation on perceptual processes. For example, reports of how the appearance of objects changes under prolonged meditation may help us to understand something about the kind of cognition involved in religious meditation.

Many of the meditation practices that have been developed within religious traditions seem to have it as one of their central functions to achieve the kind of attentiveness necessary to aesthetic, personal and religious knowing. Intrusive thoughts can interfere with all of them. Because intrusive thoughts are often related to emotional pre-occupations, the regulation of emotional states has become a central issue in following a disciplined religious path. This is something that calls for balance and subtlety. Meditation may require some degree of regulation of the expression of emotional reactions and of pre-occupation with them, but it does not require removing *awareness* of emotional reactions from consciousness. Indeed, a degree of control over the extent of emotional reactions may actually enable them to be observed more accurately, just as a professional wine-taster finds that wine can be 'tasted' better in moderation. In addition it is psychologically desirable that emotional regulation should be under-taken, if at all, in a positive and pragmatic spirit. People may *choose* to regulate emotional reactions, not because they regard them as in any way 'wrong' but simply because they interfere with meditation.

Deeper personal knowledge is both an analogue of religious knowing, and an accompaniment of it. It is possible to discern a characteristic approach to self-knowledge that is part of the religious life, an approach that is both compatible with, and analogous to, how knowledge of God is approached. Both are, in different ways, forms of religious knowing. The religious approach to self-knowledge is characterised by a sense of mystery, of patiently coming to know something deep and rather inaccessible. It contrasts, both with a lack of interest in understanding one's self at all, and also with a superficial and egoistic curiosity about oneself. Of course, it is not only among religious people that this approach to self-knowledge is promoted. However, perhaps the most important point here is that there is no conflict between seeking self-knowledge and knowledge of God. They can both be undertaken in the same spirit.

A central feature of the characteristically religious approach to self-knowledge has been an attempt to discern 'vocation', how one should lead one's life. People arrive at knowledge of their vocation in a variety of ways, the most common pattern is probably one of increasingly close approximation. The 'feedback' received from getting close is what helps them to follow the trail, feedback in terms both of personal fulfilment and a sense of following a divine purpose. It might be expected that conformity to the will of God would lead to a sense of freedom being constrained, though, characteristically, no sense of conflict is felt between the two. The crucial factor is perhaps that the relationship of the religious person with God is a cooperative relationship rather than a coercive one. Conformity to vocation arises out of a developing conceptualisation of God, the world and the self. When this conceptualisation is developed on the basis of personal experience, there is little likelihood of a sense of freedom being constrained.

In addition to the religious approach to self-knowledge there is a corresponding religious approach to the interpretation of life events. This can be discerned in prayer. Indeed prayer can be understood, at least in part, as an exercise in making sense, from a religious standpoint, of events in the world in the life of the individual person. This is a cognitive activity that can be illuminated by general cognitive psychology. For example, thanksgiving can be understood as an exercise in transforming how successes and failures are attributed. There has been much recent psychological interest in causal attributions and how they reflect peoples' mood state and influence their behaviour. Two extremes are when people are over-aware of being responsible for their successes and come to have an illusory pride, or when they are over-aware of being responsible for their failures and feel hopeless and excessively depressed. The God-centred attributions that are acquired through prayer seem to have the capacity to liberate people from both pride and depression. Confession can enable people to assimilate otherwise upsetting life events and make sense of them in terms of a broad conceptual framework. Petition can enable people to become aware of their personal needs. Even rather primitive personal needs can be acknowledged without undue distress, and metamorphosed into more mature ones in a way that parallels the maturation of needs in psychotherapy.

Prayer is an activity in which the religious person has a strong sense of his relationship to God. Human relationships provide an analogue for understanding the impact of this experienced relationship on personal knowledge and development. The religious person bases his understanding of himself partly on what he observes about his interaction with God. Similarly, parallels can be drawn between how personal growth is promoted by human relationships and by the relationship with God.

Finally, we will consider the kind of concepts that are applied to God himself. It is widely recognised that these are in some sense metaphorical concepts. For example, the concept of 'light' is applied to the natural world, but also in special ways to God. Again, there is an analogy with concepts used to describe psychological qualities. For example, in a similar way, 'strength' is applied both to physical strength and to strength of character. There is widespread agreement that such concepts are in some sense metaphorical, but considerable confusion and disagreement about what is meant by this. We will make a distinction between metaphor proper (where a concept that belongs to one domain is deliberately applied in an extended sense to another domain) and 'double-aspect' terms where concepts, such as 'light' and 'strength', have connected meanings in both the material and the psychological/spiritual domains. Some have assumed that all double-aspect terms began as metaphors, but we will argue that such evidence as is available points against this. The double-aspect terms that are applied to God may have originated, not in contrived metaphors, but in connections between material and spiritual realities that required double-aspect concepts to describe them. One implication of this view is that the double-aspect terms used to describe God cannot be expected to be open to replacement by literal language. Exactly the same issue arises with the 'mythical' stories which are central to religious thought. These are similar to double-aspect terms rather than to metaphors proper, and also cannot be expected to be amenable to 'demythologisation'. Related points can be made about the way in which the sacraments are understood. The proper comprehension of double-aspect terms lies neither in failing to distinguish the component concepts, nor in over-sophisticated interpretations that take religious concepts as *merely* symbolic. Finding a path between these extremes has been the recurrent task in understanding religious concepts and myths.

The richness of religious concepts can be affected by use, but this can go in either of two directions. Either, with frequent repetition, they can come to be used almost mindlessly and so be stripped of their original and potential resonance. Alternatively, this danger can be counteracted by a constant re-working and extension of the range of meanings embraced by core religious concepts. Many meditative practices can be seen as an exercise in preserving and extending the resonance of the ideas that are used to try to grasp the nature of the Divine presence.

This completes a brief introduction to the main themes that will be explored in the following chapters, using the framework of cognitive psychology to understand religious knowing. In the next two chapters, we will set this enterprise in the context of other attempts to understand religion from a psychological vantage-point. Empirical research on religion will be considered in chapter 2 and psychoanalytic perspectives in chapter 3.

# 2

# Psychological research on religion

One of the weaknesses of much psychological research on religion is that, in an attempt to be demonstrably objective in approach, it has concentrated exclusively on the *externals* of religion. The most commonly used measures are of belief (e.g. whether people say they believe in God) and practices (e.g. whether they go to church). This work is of only peripheral relevance to our concern with religious knowing, and we will give just a few examples to indicate the nature of this tradition of psychological research on religion. Good texts are available, containing a more detailed presentation of this work.[1] However, there are two well-established lines of research that are more relevant to religious knowing. The first concerns the development of religious thinking in children, the second concerns reports of religious experiences. We will describe an example of each in some detail.

## Studies of religious beliefs and practices

For the social psychologist, religion has five main facets:[2] the ideological (beliefs), the ritualistic (practices), the experiential (feelings), the intellectual (knowledge) and the consequential (effects). In surveys of the general population, these facets tend to be correlated with each other, and it thus appears that there is a single dimension of religiosity that underlies all of them. However, when research is conducted on people with an active religious commitment, a more subtle picture emerges. Within a religious community, a particular person can be strongly religious in one way but only weakly religious in another. For example, a series of studies by King and Hunt in the late 1960s and early 1970s[3] identified the following subcomponents of religious belief and practice: (a) *credal assent* (including variation in extent of belief in God, the Scriptures, and Christ); (b) *devotionalism* (how often a person prays); (c) *church attendance*; (d) *organisational activity* apart from worship; (e) *financial support*; (f) *religious despair/hope*; (g) *orientation to growth and striving* (including variation in the extent to which people attempt to understand and grow in faith).

A central problem for researchers in this area has been how to define religiosity. Church attendance has been the most common index of interest in religion. However, many researchers have wished to develop a more subtle measure of 'religiosity' than participation in institutional religion. The reasons for this are obvious. For example, there may be large differences in religious attitudes and experience between denominations and between different people within a denomination despite the fact that average attendance figures may be equivalent, and a method of assessing such differences is needed. More importantly, it is clear that many people who play no part in organised religion would count themselves as being 'religious' in some sense. In what way are these people the same or different from participants in institutional religion? Many scales and questionnaires have been devised which have attempted to capture 'religiosity'. In general, the larger the survey, the briefer the scale. Look, for example, at the items used by an Independent Television Authority survey in the U.K. in 1970,[4] reproduced in Table 1, items which would be viewed with some embarrassment by people interested in deeper aspects of religious belief.

This purported to measure the importance of religion to the individual. From such large scale surveys, 'degrees of religiosity' have been examined in relation to age, sex and social class. An example of such data from the ITA survey is given in Table 2.

Table 1   *Religiosity Scale Items* (from Independent Television Authority Survey 1970)

---

Individuals scored high on Religiosity if they:

(a)  classified themselves as 'very religious' or 'fairly religious'
(b)  were 'certain' that to lead a good life it is necessary to have some religious belief
(c)  were 'certain' that without belief in God life is meaningless
(d)  were 'certain' that religion helps to maintain the standard and morals of society
(e)  were 'certain' there is a God
(f)  believed that 'God does watch each person'
(g)  were 'very likely' to think of God when they are worried
(h)  were 'very likely' or 'fairly likely' to think of God when they are happy
(i)  their everyday lives were affected 'a great deal' or 'quite a lot' by their religious beliefs.

---

Table 2  *Distribution of religious attitudes by sex, age, and social class*
         *(all figures are percentages)*

|              | Religiosity | | Belief in God | |
|--------------|------|------|------|------|
|              | High | Low  | High | Low  |
| Total        | 49   | 51   | 50   | 50   |
| **Sex**      |      |      |      |      |
| Men          | 39   | 61   | 41   | 59   |
| Women        | 58   | 42   | 57   | 43   |
| **Age**      |      |      |      |      |
| 16–24        | 36   | 64   | 37   | 63   |
| 25–34        | 37   | 63   | 40   | 60   |
| 35–44        | 41   | 59   | 46   | 54   |
| 45–54        | 50   | 50   | 48   | 52   |
| 55–64        | 64   | 36   | 60   | 40   |
| 65 +         | 61   | 39   | 62   | 38   |
| **Social class** |  |      |      |      |
| AB           | 53   | 47   | 44   | 56   |
| C1           | 49   | 51   | 58   | 42   |
| C2           | 47   | 53   | 47   | 53   |
| DE           | 51   | 49   | 51   | 49   |

In addition, studies have been made of correlations between different dimensions of religiosity and denominational allegiance, type of conversion experience, personality, voting intention and intelligence.

Data on the social and psychological correlates of religious practices clearly does not get to the heart of religion. However, when such research findings are considered carefully, they can suggest more subtle conclusions than might at first be imagined. Consider, for example the finding that older people are more likely to pray.[5] Whereas only 32% of thirty-year-olds pray, the figure rises to 72% by age 70. The interpretation of this finding is not straightforward. Is it due to the fact that older people were brought up in a cultural climate in which prayer was more widely accepted, or is there a tendency for people to pray more as they get older? It is relevant here that comparable data suggests that Bible reading does *not* increase with age. Since one might expect that the early culture of older subjects would emphasise regular Bible reading as well as prayer, the absence of an increase in Bible reading with age suggests that the data for prayer may reflect real changes over the life-span. It is also intriguing that, despite the fact that praying increases with age, the belief that prayer is efficacious *declines* with age.[6] We may suppose that older subjects gradually learn that prayer has other purposes and judge its benefits on criteria other than the narrow one of its efficacy.

Perhaps the most important distinction to emerge from the last twenty years of social psychological research is that between 'committed' and 'consensual' religion.[7] Similar distinctions had already been made between the 'genuinely devout' and the 'conventionally religious'[8] and between 'intrinsic' and 'extrinsic' religion.[9] The person who is 'committed':

utilises an abstract, philosophical perspective ... religious ideas are relatively clear in meaning ... [has] ... an open and flexible framework of commitment [which] relates religion to daily activities.

By contrast, the person who is 'consensual' has a

vague, non-differentiated, bifurcated and neutralised religion, a cognitively simplified and personally convenient faith[10]

The committed/consensual distinction is important in explaining several otherwise problematic research findings. Numerous studies have found that people who are more religious are also more neurotic, racially prejudiced, anti-semitic and anti-black. Initially, it was inferred *either* that prejudiced people go to church more *or* that going to church increases racial prejudice. However, further studies have shown that such general conclusions are not warranted. In fact, *very* active church goers have very little racial prejudice. Occasional church goers, in contrast, are more prejudiced than either those who go to church regularly or those who never go.[11] Much the same has been found for neuroticism. Those who go to church occasionally have above average levels of neuroticism, whereas those who go regularly or not at all have lower than average levels.

Social psychological analyses has yielded much useful information about religion. The distinction between committed and consensual religious people has been a major advance in our thinking about the diverse characteristics of religious people. There are also many other topics, such as religious conversion, on which interesting research has been carried out. However, on its own admission, social psychology is confined to considering external aspects, to the observation of religious behaviour and the measurement of publically expressible religious attitudes.

## The development of religious thinking

Studies of the development of religious thinking in children have tended to go into greater detail about the cognitive characteristics of religious belief than the research of social psychologists on religious beliefs, and it is to work on developmental trends in religious cognition that we will now turn.

It would not be overstating the case to say that the largest influence on development psychology in this century has been Jean Piaget.[12] The four stages of development that he propounded have generated an enormous amount of psychological and educational research. It is not necessary to go into great detail about his theories, but a brief description of the main stages will be helpful as a background to understanding the development of religious concepts.

The four stages in the development of the cognitive awareness and abilities of children which he proposed are firstly, the *sensorimotor* stage lasting from birth to approximately two years characterised by the world of the young child being dominated by sensations. Towards the end of this stage, language is beginning to develop, ushering in the second stage (2–7 years) of *preoperational* thought. This stage is different from the first in that the child now has language (together with its enriched conceptual structure). The child will use objects symbolically in play (for example, blowing out a stick, pretending it is a candle). The third stage is that of concrete thought (7–11 years). Inductive and deductive logic can now be applied to concrete situations, actions, visual and sensory data. The child can thus form mental representations of actions, mental maps. These representations become more and more elaborate until, at about the age of 11 years, the final *formal operational* stage is reached. Now the young person is able to think about thought itself, generate hypotheses and apply deductive logic in an abstract way. Notice that these stages are hierarchical in the sense that each stage incorporates the last. Although the ages at which one stage gives way to the next may differ from child to child, nevertheless the progression will always tend to be through one stage to the next.

These stages can be illustrated by changes in children's approach to history. At the preoperational stage this is characterised by rote learning. Reality is mixed with fantasy, the major distinction in the child's mind being between 'present' and 'absent', so that dragons (absent) and William I of England (absent) are categorised together. In the concrete operational stage, the major distinction changes from present/absent to true/false. The child seeks to classify events on the basis of whether they 'really happened' or could 'really happen today'. The ability to make transitive inferences allows children to understand historical sequence, and they are able to begin to discern shifts in historical civilisations. At the stage of formal operations (11 + ), the child can abstract general properties of civilisations, and can follow the progress of a people over time, comparing past and present interpretations of events. One can thus see how changes in a child's concept of history relate to the general development of cognitive abilities.

Does religious understanding develop along similar lines? Preliminary observations suggest that it does. Before the age of three the child is absorbing the basic intellectual and emotional patterns of behaviour. Most psychologists would call this a 'prereligious' phase. During the preoperational stage, the child shows fairy-tale conceptions of God and of Bible stories. This is partly due to a strong animistic tendency in younger children (around five years of age) so that, for example, the clouds move 'because God pushes them', and partly due to the dominance of the present/absent distinction to which we have already made reference. The question of the presence or absence of God arises for a young child in the same way as for giants ('are there giants in those caves?') and greater awe is due to God merely because he is 'greater'; 'bigger' and 'better'. The six year old can however grasp the idea of God as creator of the world and of the beautiful things it contains. The 'concrete operational' child's concern with truth and falsehood allows a more sceptical approach: 'Where is heaven?' 'Why can't you see God?' 'How can he be everywhere?' 'Is He inside me?' More advanced use of symbols allow the child to grasp the idea of God as 'father', and an increasing awareness of sequencing in history allow him or her to set Bible stories in some historical context. Finally, around the age of eleven, the beginning of 'propositional' thinking allows an individualistic approach in which concepts of God vary from conventional to mystical.

There has been a substantial body of research concerned with the development of religious thinking in children,[13] but perhaps the most famous is Ronald Goldman's attempt in the 1960s to apply such Piagetian constructs to the child's understanding of religion.[14] He used Bible stories and pictures of religious activities (e.g. people going into a church) to probe children's concepts of religion on six dimensions: God (His nature and power, what 'holiness' meant); man's relationship to God (guilt, fears, trust; demands of divine love and justice; how the divine communicates with man); group man in relation to God (divine love and justice in relation to a group);

concepts of Jesus (his humanity, power and relationship with God); concepts of miracles (God's power over nature, divine intervention); and biblical authority (relevance of Bible for today).

His conclusion that one must be very cautious in teaching Bible stories (especially from Old Testament) to the under-11s have been hotly debated, so it is worth looking at the methods and results on which these conclusions are based. We shall concentrate here on his Bible story research. Some other aspects of his work will be discussed in subsequent chapters. In pilot research, he used eight stories from the Bible which he found to be used in Religious Instruction syllabuses in infant (5–7), junior (8–11) and secondary (11 +) schools. From this pilot research he found that children's responses to just three of the stories illustrated the conceptual structure they brought to bear on all the stories. These three were Moses and the burning bush; the crossing of the Red Sea; and the temptations of Jesus. He used these stories as the basis of interviews with 60 children aged 6, 9, 13, and 16 years.

He found that between the ages of five and nine, God is seen as physical, anthropomorphic (e.g. having a 'voice', literally), living in 'heaven' which is located in the sky, though His visitations are rare now compared with Biblical times. He possesses magical powers and employs them somewhat unpredictably, like a touchy adult. Naughty people are punished. 'Jesus' and 'God' are often confused.

Between the ages of nine and twelve, 'God' comes to have supernatural rather than superhuman attributes, though some physical attributes ('voice' and 'power') are maintained. A gulf begins to open between 'scientific' and theological explanations for events. The concept of 'guilt' develops and a 'problem of evil' starts to present itself as an 'all loving' God is believed in. Miracles are given magical explanations. Some children begin to see that the Bible may deal with current issues.

After the age of thirteen, God is conceived in terms of symbolic, abstract and spiritualised ideas, and fewer anthropomorphic ideas are found. The 'voice' of God is seen as an analogy. God is seen as loving all men (including 'evil' men). The young person is now able to understand the Biblical narrative in terms of developing purpose in Israel's destiny, and able to understand the subjective elements of the struggle between good and evil in the temptation story.

The critical feature which Goldman extrapolated from these data (expanded in his later book *Readiness for Religion*)[15] was the literalism shown before the eleven to thirteen age period. Taking, for example, the Red Sea story, in the early years God is seen as personally involved, physically causing the waves to separate. In the second stage, God makes it happen by supernatural means, rather than causing it Himself. In the third stage, rational explanations are offered (though only after a period of confusion as a material explanation seems to compete with the 'authority' of the Bible). For the teenagers in Goldman's study, God was involved by 'putting it into the minds of the Israelites to make use of naturally occurring sea-crossing conditions'. Goldman's point is that the younger children tend to focus on concrete and irrelevant aspects of the story. This emphasis on trivialities, and on a crude idea of God's material intervention may actually *arrest* development, producing later mis-understanding and rejection of the whole because these parts are seen as untenable. A secondary, less potent, criticism of early Bible teaching is that constant retelling (in order to allow the more sophisticated concepts to emerge) will cause the stories to lose their drama.

It is possible to criticise Goldman's research on methodological grounds. He used a 'cross sectional' design, (studying different children at different ages) to draw conclusions about changes that occur in any *individual* child over time. Also, he drew conclusions about the effects of telling Bible stories to young children without studying a 'control' group of children who had not been exposed to early Bible stories, nor a control group of children who had been exposed to Biblical teaching of a less 'literal' nature. Furthermore, there is, to this day, no evidence that repetition of stories does any damage to childrens' religious development. Subsequent investi-gations have also pointed out that too much weight was put on childrens' interpretation of too few stories, interpretations of which were elicited by asking questions which may themselves have led to curious answers. For example, if a young child is asked 'If Moses had looked at God, what do you think he would have seen?', he or she is likely to supply an answer, even if the question would not have arisen spontaneously. To be fair, Goldman mentions some of these criticisms and deals with them himself.

His research remains important, not least because it avoids being reductionist; it never suggests that religious understanding is reducible to psychological phenomena. Rather, it illustrates in a very direct way how general psychological functioning can affect religious under-standing. It is an exercise in 'mapping' religious thinking on to what we know more generally about cognitive processes.

We may also infer that if these stages are valid descriptions of children's development, then they are also likely to describe aspects of adult conceptions of God, since it is assumed that each subsequent stage *incorporates* rather than replaces the former. That is, we may all, under certain circumstances (e.g. under stress) conceive of God in a cruder, materialistic way, indignant because He seems to punish the good and let the evil men go free (indignant because it is inconsistent with our earliest notions of God who punishes the naughty and rewards the good). Indeed the lasting benefit of Goldman's researches may well be the insight they give into levels of adult experiences of God and some of these are explored further in chapters 8 (on prayer) and 9 (on concepts of God).

## *Psychological studies of religious experience*

Finally, we come to the study of religious experience itself. Most investigations have used questionnaire methods to elicit reports of such experiences, and have then examined what sort of people report such experiences.

A major aspect which has been investigated has been whether organised religion is necessarily the place to look if one is seeking mystical experience. William James in 1902 was inclined to be sceptical of the prospect:

A genuine first hand religious experience ... is bound to be a heterodoxy to its witnesses, the prophet appearing as a mere lonely madman. If his doctrine proves contagious enough to spread to any others, it becomes a definite and labeled heresy. But, if it then still proves contagious enough to triumph over persecution, it becomes itself an orthodoxy; and when religion has become an orthodoxy, its way of inwardness is over; the spring is dry; the faithful live at second hand exclusively and stone prophets in their turn.[16]

Is this mere caricature, or can empirical study support it?

The following commonly asked questions have been used in the questionnaires or structured interviews to investigate mystical or religious experience.[17]

Have you ever had an experience:

— in which all things seemed to be unified into a single whole
— of tremendous personal expansion, either psychological or physical
— in which time, place and distance were meaningless
— in which you realised your oneness with all things
— of holiness
— of deep and profound peace
— which could not be put adequately into words
— in which a new view of reality was revealed to you

— in which all was felt to be perfection at that time
— in which everything seemed to disappear from your mind until you were conscious only of a void?

A perennial problem for research on mystical experience is what criteria to use in determining whether such an experience actually took place. Seeing one's child being born, being totally embarrassed by forgetting a dinner engagement, sexual orgasm: each of these contain elements that 'cannot be put into words', yet would not normally be considered a mystical experience. Stace identified five core aspects which other researchers have since adopted as criteria:[18]

(a) the experience is *noetic* or perceived as a valid sort of knowledge; not merely 'subjective' or 'emotional';
(b) the experience is *ineffable* or not describable in words;
(c) the experience is *holy* or 'religious' but not tied to any particular theological construction;
(d) the experience is associated with *positive feeling* or perceived as a profound, pleasurable experience, yet not arising merely from pleasant emotion;
(e) the experience is *paradoxical*, defying logic.

Stace added four extra criteria, the first two relating to what he called 'extrovertive mysticism'

(f) a feeling that, in some sense, all things are 'alive' and
(g) a feeling that all things are *one*; distinct, yet part of a whole.

The final two related to 'introvertive mysticism':

(h) the feeling of timelessness and spacelessness
(i) a feeling of 'void': a perfect unity of consciousness devoid of any content; a dissolution of sense of self.

In fact, subsequent research[19] has shown that a clear distinction between introvertive and extrovertive experience cannot be sustained. Rather, there appear to be two elements to the experience – a 'pure experience' factor (consisting of phenomena of timelessness, spacelessness, ineffability, unity) and an 'interpretive' factor (consisting of aspects which may be more derivative or context-bound such as holiness, positive feelings, noetic quality). Although these two aspects are distinguishable, they nevertheless tend to occur together. The *contexts* in which they occur have occupied psychologists since James' comments that organised religion tends to stifle such experience.

Indeed, early research tended to support the idea that increased 'religiosity' (conventionally defined) tended to be associated with *fewer* reports of mystical-type experiences. This paradoxical finding is reminiscent of the apparent associations between religiosity and prejudice discussed above. There it was noted that both people who were very committed to religion (in terms of participation in religious practices) and people who were not at all committed to religion showed less prejudice than those who were 'conventionally religious', attending religious services infrequently. An exactly similar relationship exists for the association of mystical experience and commitment to religious practice. The research of Ralph Hood[20] has confirmed that more frequent Church attenders have higher rates of mystical experience than less frequent attenders, but not higher than nonattenders. Once again we see the importance of distinguishing between 'committed' and 'consensual' manifestations of religion. It should also be noted that many people of no religious affiliation report religious experiences.

Of course, in large scale survey research, it is not often possible to go into much detail, and one or two questions such as 'have you ever had an experience that you cannot put into words' are used. Such general survey questions may then be followed up with more intensive research at a later date. The work of David Hay[21] is a good example of this research strategy. He and his colleagues started out with survey research methods, having an opinion poll company asking people in the street the following question:

*Have you ever been aware of, or influenced by, a presence or power, whether you call it God or not, which is different from your everyday self?*

There was some prior research which had indicated that this was a question to which a substantial minority would say 'yes'. Gallup polls in the USA in the 1960s had reported about 30% of people admitting to having had 'religious or mystical experience − sudden religious awakening or insight'. More recently, Greeley[22] had found that 35% said 'yes' to a question about the experience of being 'close to a powerful, spiritual force that seemed to lift you out of yourself'. In Hay's 1976 survey in the United Kingdom, a broadly comparable 31% of positive responses were found to this question, and a higher figure of 36% answered the broader question about 'being aware of or influenced by a presence or power'. This proportion of just over a third contained slightly more women (41%) than men (31%). There was a tendency for older people to report more experiences, and Hay argues that this is due to a decreasing interest in religion among young people in the United Kingdom rather than to the fact that older people have had more opportunities to have such experiences in their lives.

Hay followed up his general survey by taking a random sample of local people and interviewing them in their own homes. Under these conditions, he found a higher proportion (62%) who said they had experienced being aware of a presence or power. We shall first give a brief outline of his main findings.

Nine categories of religious experience were identified: (a) the presence of God, (b) answered prayer, (c) a presence not named, (d) nature mysticism, (e) the presence of the dead, (f) premonitions, (g) meaningful patterning of events, (h) conversion (a rather small category) and, (i) evil powers (experiences during seances or use of ouija boards).

The feature all these have in common is that it was not merely intellectual appreciation of some state of affairs that was being reported upon, but an intense and profound experience which seemed somehow more 'real' than everyday commonplace reality. This greater reality was sometimes identified with God, and sometimes not, depending on the previous interests and interpretations of the individual having the experience. For example, in the first category, 'the presence of God', Hay reports a woman saying

Something woke me up. There was something or somebody by my bed; I wasn't frightened. Within ten minutes the torment I'd felt, for some strange reason left me. I think I had more peace than I'd had for a very long time … I have enough knowledge to know that there's somebody there, to know that I need never be so alone again … he decided I needed help.[23]

This account illustrates themes which recur. Such experiences come unexpectedly, last a fairly short time (seconds or minutes rather than hours), often occur against the background of intense distress (50% of people who had such an experience were distressed or confused before it occurred) and occur when the person is alone (66% were completely alone, others were alone but in a public place; only a small minority occurred in a communal setting). Hay found that reports of such experiences occurring within public worship are rather rare, though the findings of other researchers are not altogether consistent on this point.[24] Similar experiences were reported by people who do not relate their experience to God.

It was just about dark and I was looking out of the library window … I was aware of everything going on around me – and I felt very alone. But at the same time I was aware of something that was giving me strength and keeping me going … protecting me.[25]

Here the feeling of 'aloneness' is present although things are happening around the person. This is clearly very different from the heightened expressions of emotion commonly observed in large religious revival meetings. They are quiet, profound, and more solitary. Although they commonly occur 'out of the blue', many individuals have discovered situations (e.g. being in surroundings of natural beauty or practising meditation) that are conducive to such experiences.

About five years ago, sitting on a mountain top in the middle of Dartmoor... I felt that I wasn't alone − it came quite suddenly ... I've been doing some TM recently and I find occasionally ... there's a feeling of being part of a whole. It is a very physical awareness of myself as an organism which relates to a greater organism.[26]

The effect of these experiences is more often positive than negative. Only 15% reported being 'alarmed', and a further 12% were 'confused', but 61% felt at peace, 'restored', happy, or uplifted and awestruck. Three-quarters of the people who reported such experiences or such an experience felt it had changed their outlook in some way, confirming or intensifying belief, making them more optimistic, giving insight into life or encouraging moral behaviour.

Hay found that people had rarely told anyone else about the experience until specifically asked about it in the context of the interview. They supposed that their family and friends would not understand, or would think they were going insane. Hay likens this to previous taboos surrounding sexual matters. One person had attempted to discuss her experience with a clergyman, only to find that he seemed not to understand what she was talking about. 'There seems to be a feeling that "society" in some way does not give permission for these experiences to be integrated into ordinary life.'[27]

Why are such experiences not integrated into ordinary life despite the increase in interest in Eastern approaches to mind (evident in classes in yoga and meditation available throughout the United Kingdom)? It is interesting to note two things about these developments. Firstly there has been a relative neglect of Western tradition of contemplative religion and mysticism. Secondly, where the meditation approaches of the East have been adopted, they have often been seen, in characteristically 'Western style', as techniques to help to achieve some goal (reduce stress, give up smoking, lose weight, get fit). All of these may be worthy aims, but they tend to ignore the central aspect of the meditative experience itself. Despite increased interest in meditation, and despite the fact that many people persist in *believing* that some divine dimension exists (as every survey suggests is the case, even though there has been a reduction in institutional religious activity), people who have experience of an 'other' dimension feel that they cannot openly discuss the experience for fear of being misunderstood. These experiences should be taken more seriously by mainstream theologians and psychologists than has hitherto been the case.

The central question about such religious experiences in the context of this book is what contribution they make to religious knowing. They are clearly not a sufficient condition for religious knowing. The fact that many non-religious people report similar experiences appears to provide clear support for this point. What is particularly interesting is exactly how religious people move from the raw experience itself to a religious articulation of that experience. We will argue in chapter 5 that it is a process rather like that which occurs when patients in psychotherapy move from 'felt meanings' to articulated personal insights.

# 3

## Psychoanalytic approaches to religious experience

Psychoanalytic studies of religion are not open to the charge that can be made against much survey research on religion of having concentrated on externals. Psychoanalysis has concerned itself with the psychological origins of religion. However, it has often appeared to press reductionist explanations of religious phenomena, to explain religion away in psychological terms. Freud's approach was not only reductionist but openly unsympathetic to religion. Nevertheless, it has long been clear that there is nothing in psychoanalysis that is intrinsically hostile to religion and no reason why psychoanalysis need advance reductionist explanations of it. After an initial consideration of Freud we will review the approach of Jung, whose explicit sympathy with religion is well known, and also consider the work of a group of contemporary psychoanalytic theorists whose approach to religion has been influenced by Donald Winnicott.

### Freud (1856–1939)

Freud's views on religion fall into two separate though related groups – one about the origins of religious thought in the development of mankind, and one about the origins of religious thought in the individual person. These two aspects map neatly onto his two major writings on the subject: *Totem and Taboo* (1913)[1] which examines the first, and *The Future of an Illusion* (1927)[2] which examines the second. (His third book on a religious theme: *Moses and Monotheism* (1939)[3] largely restates and applies the theories developed in his early work to the figure of Moses and will not be considered here.) The heart of the 'reductionist' thesis is found in the 1927 book but these ideas are more clearly understood in the light of the earlier *Totem and Taboo*. Our discussion of Freud's views will necessarily be brief; fuller accounts can be found in books by Ricœur[4] or Meissner.[5]

In *Totem and Taboo*, Freud attempted to explain the religious behaviour of 'primitive' people with the help of observations of neurotic patients. The book is in four parts and it is in the fourth section that particular links are drawn between the setting apart of the totem animal as taboo and incest taboo. The theory is that the taboo derives from sexual relationships between members of the same tribe, the totem animal representing the father of the tribe or clan or family. The father figure is one who, by his presence, denies sexual access to members of the same tribe. At some point in prehistory the father had exclusive power of disposal over the women in the tribe. The sons had organised a coup and killed him, but thereafter nursed this secret and its guilt. This ancient theme occurs again in the Oedipus myth. Totemism involves the sexual taboo of all women within the same totem tribe, the sons being unable to be free towards the father's women. At the totem feast where the totem animal is ceremoniously eaten, grief and joy combine in what is really a symbolic reenactment of the father's murder. Religion has its origin in this event, has guilt as its major motivating force, and results in ritualistic practices as attempts to expiate the guilt.

The neurotic manifestation most often used by Freud as the model for the behaviour of 'primitive' tribes and of modern religious ceremony is the obsessional patient. This form of neurosis is associated with the fear of touching certain things for fear of contamination, or the constant fear that one has done something dangerous without realising it. An obsessional patient might spend some hours washing his hands and face in a stereotyped way to get rid of the feeling of being dirty, or may make exhaustive, repetitive and unnecessary checks to ensure he has not left gas taps on, left doors unlocked, or left stones or pieces of wood on the pavement that others may trip over.

What then are the key elements in religion? Freud believes them to be the veneration of a father figure (God, Jesus), the belief in the power of the Spirit or Spirits, and the rituals of religion. The veneration of the father figure has its origins in childhood, when the child in the oedipal phase deals with anxiety about the possibility of punishment by the father by venerating him, identifying with him, and introjecting his will in the form of the superego. The power of spirit is reminiscent of the belief in magic found in both primitive tribes and children, and the ritual is merely shared obsessional behaviour, performed to deal with the shared guilt about killing the father − Jesus? − and even Moses (since Freud argues in *Moses and Monotheism* that Moses was murdered!).

Freud's line of argument is thus clear. He studied obsessional patients in some detail (his analysis of the 'Wolf Man' was particularly influential) and believed that he saw in them the result of unresolved childhood stages, particularly the 'anal' stage where the child first learns associations between guilt and being 'unclean'. He identified elements of the religious ritual of primitive tribes and in current religious practice (such as ritual cleansing ceremonies), which he believed resembled obsessional patients' vain attempts to rid themselves of the contamination and/or guilt, and he suggested that they share similar origins, the repression of aggressive feelings. Furthermore they have an Oedipal quality – they are centred on aggression towards, and subsequent veneration of the father figure.

Before considering how this argument is developed to explain the origins of religious thought in the individual, it is interesting that Freud's theories about the origin of religious thought in the species suffer from many problems. Let us briefly mention three. Firstly, he infers how things used to be in the ancestry of mankind by observing 'primitive' culture of his own day. Although it may be legitimate to make comparisons between different cultures of their *current* behaviour and thought patterns, it is not legitimate to assert that one of the comparison groups gives an insight as to how things once were with the other. Secondly, Freud made inferences about beliefs of 'primitive' peoples on the basis of only some parts of their behaviour. Take for example, 'magical' belief in the power of spirits to produce rain for the crops. Observing only a piece of ceremony or ritual, it may be inferred that people believed that such ritual was both a necessary and sufficient cause for the crops to grow. But why do the rituals occur at the season when rain is expected, and why does 'primitive' man also till the soil, sow the seed and water the land? If you observed only these agricultural efforts and ignored the rituals you might infer that physical cause-and-effect relationships were correctly understood. Thirdly, Freud made the error of arbitrary part-whole inference. He concentrated on limited resemblances between behaviours in two separate domains (for example, between purification ceremonies and obsessional handwashing) and ignored many dissimilarities. Obsessional patients often have anxiety provoking ruminations which they feel controlled by, and cannot neutralise. These obsessional aspects are absent from most religions. Also, some religions have very little ritual, and no purification ceremonies.

When Freud turned to the origins of religion in the individual man (*The Future of an Illusion*), he saw parallels with its development in the species. Religion preserves for the adult (c.f. contemporary man) a piece of infantile behaviour (c.f. primitive culture). The heart of Freud's reductionist thesis is that religion is an immature response to the awareness of helplessness, an illusion created as a way of coping with unpleasant reality ... 'my father will protect me, he is in control'. God is thus seen as an 'ideal' father figure, a *projection* of a person's own mind. As we have seen, religious belief for Freud involves fixation at both the anal and oedipal phases. The anal influence gives it an obsessional character, the emphasis on ritual, orderliness and cleanness. The oedipal influence gives it the 'relationship' to the father — all-powerful, to be feared and also to be loved. Other writers have stressed the way in which Freud was a child of his time, expressing the idealism of the enlightenment. For many thinkers in the nineteenth century, 'reason' was all, and a positivistic scientific view of reality was all-pervasive in their discussion of man's beliefs and behaviours. (Compare Feuerbach's explanation of behaviour in instinctual terms, and Marx's explanation in economic terms.) Religion to Freud is functional, and its function is to create an illusion to reduce fears of helplessness.

Perhaps the most abiding aspect of Freud's reductionist theory is the contention that God is a projection of an ideal father figure. It is the aspect of Freud's theories about religion which is most often quoted by those who wish to undermine the claims made by theistic religions that they deal with realities. As we shall see, in as far as it can be tested significantly at all, Freud's theory is wrong; while other aspects of it are in principle untestable.

The first problem is to know what evidence to take as indicating that projection has taken place. It could be argued that projection would result in 'God' and 'one's father' having shared characteristics. On the other hand, if no shared characteristics are found, this might be because one is projecting the ideal father one *didn't* have! In fact when psychologists have examined peoples' descriptions of 'God', they have found that they overlap more with people's concept of 'mother' than 'father'.[6] Where overlaps *do* exist between personal concepts of 'God' and 'father' this only occurs when the father is the preferred parent. The pattern of results suggest a more mundane explanation than 'projection'. If one makes ratings of *any* well-loved person, object or even pet animal on scales such as 'likeable—unlikeable', 'loving—hateful', 'friendly—distant', 'kind—cruel', one tends to find that they are rated similarly. Well-liked friends, members of one's family, pets, foods and teddy-bears tend to be rated positively. So even the modest similarities that exist between peoples' concepts of 'God' and their 'parents' may exist not because of projection but because they are both valued 'personalities'. From any demonstration that one object is similar to another, one cannot infer that one is a projection of the other.

Note, then, that the core of the reductionist 'projection' theory can itself be explained in more plausible psychological terms. Many problems arise because Freud did not base his theories on the sort of careful observation of behaviour which characterises some of his most valuable contributions to other aspects of abnormal psychology. Specifically, Freud did not derive his theories about the development of religion by observing how that development actually took place in children. His ideas about religion are derived from superficial similarities between certain religious beliefs and practices and some forms of *adult* neuroses. Since his analytic theory supposed that adult neuroses were derived from childhood conflicts, he concluded that religious belief must have a similar origin.

Neither were his theories based on any exhaustive observation of religious beliefs and practices. Had he made such observations he would have found that religious practices differed markedly from one religion to another. Oriental religions, for example, do not emphasise the father figure. The amount of ritual differs between religions and within religions. Indeed, one may have as much difficulty defining religious belief and practices as Wittgenstein had in defining what the word 'game' referred to; and one might well conclude that different religions, like different games, merely share some family resemblances. Freud's problem was that he took one or two family members to be representative of the whole family, took one or two aspects of the behaviour of these family members (which were similar to neurosis) to be the central aspects of religion, and then inferred the same cause for each.

In fact, Freud realised that the projection theory of God did not entail that God did not exist. In a letter to his friend, the German pastor Oskar Pfister, on 26 November 1927, Freud wrote

Let me be quite clear on the point that the views expressed in my book form no part of analytic theory. They are my personal views ... if I drew on analysis for certain arguments, that need deter no one from using the nonpartisan method of analysis for arguing the opposite view.[7]

## Jung (1875–1961)

The attitude of Jung to religion differs in many ways from Freud's, though his approach grew out of psychoanalysis and retained some of its assumptions. His evident sympathy with religion, and his attempt to escape from the reductionist approach to it, make his views of particular interest. However, on neither point is his position quite as straightforward as it seems at first sight. There are a number of issues on which he is ambivalent and he makes statements that are not easy to reconcile. Also, his views on religion changed very considerably from the early views set out in *Psychology of the Unconscious* (1911–12)[8] to his last major book on religion, *Answer to Job* (1951),[9] though probably the best single exposition of his position is the opening essay entitled 'Introduction to the Religious and Psychological Problem of Alchemy' published in 1944 in Jung's *Psychology and Alchemy*.[10] Heisig has provided a scholarly account of the development of Jung's changing views on God.[11]

Unlike Freud, Jung grew up in a 'religious' household, being the son of a Swiss pastor..Ironically, however, it was in the rejection of his father's rationalistic approach to religion (an approach which Freud might have applauded) which helped frame many of his ideas about what the core elements of religion are. After studying medicine he specialised in psychiatry and became interested in the structure and activity of the unconscious, especially as revealed by dreams. He became friendly with Freud, and they visited the United States together in 1909 (Freud was 53 and Jung 34). But it was a relationship which was not to last, partly because of their different views, partly because of their different personalities.

Jung's views on religion in *Psychology of the Unconscious*, written towards the end of his brief association with Freud, are close to Freud's on many points, though his greater sympathy with religion is already evident. He shared Freud's idea that the image of God is a projection from the unconscious, and that the personal history of an individual is the main determinant of whether and in what form such a projection arises. However, as his views developed, he emphasised increasingly the source of the image of God in the collective unconscious. Unfortunately Jung's definition of the collective unconscious is elusive. At some points he makes only modest claims for the concept (that it is the sum of primordial experiences of mankind, a form of 'race memory'). At other times, and especially later on in his life, it became a sort of supra-material, shared consciousness. For example, he used it to explain how he could have a quasi-hallucinatory image of someone who was subsequently discovered to have died somewhere else at the very moment the image was seen.

In emphasising the collective unconscious as the source of the image of God he was making a less radical departure from Freud's views than is sometimes supposed, as Freud also suggested that as a person's concept of God develops 'the ideational image belonging to his childhood is ... merged with the inherited memory traces of the primal father'.[12] Exactly how the concept of the primal father was supposed to be inherited is not much clearer in Freud that it is in Jung. However, they diverged over exactly what is inherited. For Freud, it seems to have been the *content* of the primal father. Jung, in contrast, thought it was more plausible that it was a 'form' or 'pattern', a kind of abstract schema that was inherited, and that this was then fleshed out by the individual with specific content drawn from his own experience. This inherited schema is essentially what Jung meant by an 'archetype', one of the key concepts of his analytical psychology. Unfortunately this concept, too, is difficult to define.[13] The essential difficulty is whether it is merely a descriptive concept, or whether it is meant to *explain* anything.

This general issue arises in a particular form regarding the representation of God in the psyche. Let us accept for the sake of argument that the image of God does arise from the unconscious, and that collective elements feature prominently in this, together with personal ones. The key question that remains is whether God actually exists independently of the God-image in the psyche. Jung says repeatedly through his writings that this is not a question for him as a psychologist using empirical methods. All he can do is to study the image of God as he finds it in the psyche; it is not for him to decide whether it is a reflection of an actual God. That would be a metaphysical rather than a psychological question.

On the face of things this sounds a very reasonable approach, but Jung pleased neither psychologists nor theologians by it. Part of the trouble is that, though he reiterates this position, he also departs from it. At times he shows apparent hostility to the idea of a 'metaphysical' God as he is inclined to call it. There are times, even well on in his life, when he appears to say, not just that he, as a psychologist, cannot comment on the existence of God, but that no one is in a position to hold that God exists as a separate, metaphysical entity. At other times he gives the impression that he does, of course, believe in the existence of God, but that it is only the image of God in the psyche that he can actually demonstrate scientifically. Both theists and atheists can find many passages in the corpus of Jung's writings to which they can take fierce exception.

Apart from his inconsistency, another source of difficulty is his philosophy of knowledge. Jung declared his philosophical allegiance to Kant, finding congenial the notion that experience is mediated through mental categories. One conclusion he draws from this is that we can never know 'things in themselves', but only know them as we experience them. This provides a buttress for his view that we can never know a metaphysical God, but only know Him as he is reflected in our mental life. In a parallel way, he makes a distinction between the manifestations of an archetype in particular individuals and the unknown archetype that stands behind it. However, there is an inconsistency in Jung over how the archetypes fit into this Kantian epistemology. The archetypes seem to be both *categories* through which experience is filtered, but also transcendental *objects*. This ambiguity is never resolved.

Leaving aside the question of the *status* of God, Jung also makes major departures from Freud over the psychic functions served by the image of God. Freud was concerned to trace projections of God back to their sources in the personal history of particular individuals. The projection had no constructive function other than its role in dealing with an unresolved psychic problem. Jung did not wholly reject this way of looking at images of God, but he certainly regarded it as incomplete. He also saw the image of God as pointing the way forward towards a person's individuation (wholeness and fulfilment), and as being a mediator between consciousness and unconsciousness.

The concept of the numinous, the experience of the divine as a fascinating and awesome mystery, developed in Rudolf Otto's *The Idea of the Holy*[14] encapsulated Jung's view of religious images. The core of Jung's philosophy is that man is naturally religious. At some point in a person's development he or she will become aware of the numinous aspect of their own unconscious and will have to respond to it. It should perhaps be noted here that almost anything numinous belongs, for Jung, to the world of religion and speaks of 'God'. Though the criteria for what is to be treated as reflecting the image of God are not wholly clear, they are certainly exceedingly broad.

So, Jung does not attack the transcendent concept of God, but suggests how man can have a clearer understanding of the immanent aspect of God. It is implicit that as the nature of 'consciousness' of man changes through the ages, so people will need to rediscover God through the archetype of God in their own unconscious. Since dogmas and creeds are intellectual attempts to capture truths, they are likely to be more culture-dependent and relative to the cultured context in which they were proposed, and less meaningful to other cultures and ages. As such, they may demand correction and restatement so that the archetypal truths they contain may again be made available.

Jung's view of the God-image as a symbol of, and pointer towards, the state of individuation led him increasingly to see the Self as an image of God. 'Self', as we shall see in more detail in chapter 7, is used in an unusual way by Jung to refer to the whole person, including as yet unrealised potential and unconscious contents. This represents another break with Freud's view of God as a father-figure. Jung was sufficiently sympathetic to Christianity to regard Christ as a particularly powerful symbol of the Self, though some of his followers such as James Hillman[15] have not been persuaded that there is any necessary connection between Jung's archetypal psychology and Christianity, or even monotheism.

Jung's work is attractive on account of his detailed and sympathetic consideration of religion, and his attempt to break away from Freudian reductionism. But it would be unwise to make the simple assumption that Jung's theories are *pro* religion and Freud's are *contra*. It is certainly the case that their personal views differed markedly in the seriousness with which they took religious experience. There have, however, been influential psychoanalytic writers who refuse to conclude from this that the theories themselves are to be so easily dichotomised as *pro* and *contra*. Fromm (1950) for example has persuasively argued that Freud's aims have more in common with the aims of religion than have Jung's.[16] For Freud's aim was enlightenment, the pursuit of truth, and freedom from the slavery of the fixations to aspects of the past. Psychoanalysis, as practised by Freud, aimed to encourage the individual to strive for truth and freedom, especially freedom from neurotically incestuous ties with other people, with a tribe, a party or a state. Fromm argues that it is the hallmark of all the major religions that they also encourage this transition from 'incest' and dependence to freedom and independence. He therefore rejects the Jungian approach, arguing that it reduces religion to psychological phenomena and elevates the unconscious to a religious phenomenon. Such relativism, he maintains, looks at first sight to be more approachable, but on closer examination is fundamentally opposed to Judaism, Christianity and Buddhism.

Fromm's arguments are interesting, and have been influential in encouraging people to take a new look at the implications of Freud's writings. But we must also see his views in context. Firstly, Fromm believes that religious experience is deeply rooted in man, belonging to his nature *per se*. On this, he is closer to Jung than to Freud. Religion helps man find unity in living. The question is not whether or not an individual has a religion, but *which* religion he has, what are the ultimate goals which give meaning to his life. Allegiances to money, ideologies or the state can all seem as religions. This makes it clear why Fromm rejects the Jungian approach which strives to 'incorporate' the religious aspects of man into psychoanalysis. Fromm included allegiances to the state as a religion, and the rise of the Nazis in Germany were still recent as he wrote a book which was published only five years after the end of the second World War. Freud's theories, which emphasised the emancipation from religion in its neurotic and incestuous aspects, were thus more congenial to Fromm. Jung's counter to Fromm would be that it is precisely when man imagines that he can eliminate the numinous that it is likely to break out in the uncontrolled form that occurred in Nazi Germany.

Jung's theories are problematic on several grounds other than those indicated by Fromm. His concept of religion is so broad, and at times so heterodox, that it is not clear how closely it relates to what is ordinarily understood by religion. Secondly, though he broke away from Freud's explanation of the idea of God as a projection from the person's unconscious, it seems that he may have simply offered an alternative explanation of God as a projection from the collective unconscious. Whether this is a correct interpretation depends on whether or not the collective unconscious is treated as an explanatory concept, and on this, as we have seen, he vacillates. If it is to be taken as an explanation of the experience of God in the psyche, then his Kantian epistemology would lead him to argue that what explains our experience of God can never itself be known. This is a scientifically unattractive proposal, though it is not necessary to take the collective unconscious as an explanatory concept.

Despite its problems and weaknesses, Jung's contribution to the study of religious experience is pioneering and massive, and we shall refer to it at several points during this book.

### Contemporary psychoanalytic approaches to religion

Psychoanalytic theory has been far from static during the decades since Freud's own work, and has led to a re-appraisal of religion within the psychoanalytic tradition. Developments in basic psychoanalytic theory have combined with a more subtle understanding of religious phenomena to make possible a burgeoning of sympathetic and fruitful psychoanalytic work on religion.

In Freudian theory, there is an underlying dichotomy between the 'pleasure' principle and the 'reality' principle. Freud had a strong, personal commitment to 'reality', and a deep hostility to outcroppings of pleasure-seeking, which he regarded as psychologically immature. For all that Freud served to foster an emancipation of the sexual morality of Western society, he was in many ways a stern moralist. Religious ideas, which he saw as reflecting wish fulfilment, were on the side of the pleasure principle and in opposition to the reality principle; hence his iconoclastic opposition to religion.

However, religion, like all human phenomena, can take many forms, varying in their psychological maturity. It can readily be conceded that some of these forms represent an immature retreat from uncongenial aspects of external reality into a comforting, self-contained world of religious beliefs and practices. But is this necessarily true of all forms of religion? This was one of the points with which Freud's friend, Oskar Pfister took issue in the debate[17] that surrounded publication of *The Future of an Illusion*.[18] Pfister, like Freud, was on the side of realistic thinking rather than wishful thinking. Freud saw religion as being based on 'illusions, fulfilments of the oldest, strongest and more urgent wishes of mankind'. Pfister countered that 'the gentleness and humility, the self-denial and rejection of riches, the sacrifice of his own life for the highest moral values — in short, the entire standard of life that the crucified of Golgotha demands of his followers — is diametrically opposed to the lusts of primitive nature'.

André Godin has extended this line of argument in an excellent recent psychoanalytic study of religion.[19] At the heart of his argument is the claim that the Christian, by identifying with Christ's wishes for him, rather than with his own psychic needs, is on the side of the reality principle rather than the pleasure principle.

However, there has been a growing awareness in psychoanalytic theory that the dichotomy that Freud erected between fantasy and reality is too sharp. The work of Donald Winnicott[20] on the 'transitional sphere' has been particularly important here and has provided the basis for a new wave of psychoanalytic theories of religion. Winnicott's own remarks on religion are no more than brief indications but others, notably Pruyser,[21] Rizzuto[22] and Meissner[23] have developed his ideas in a way that is important for our concern with the nature of religious knowing. Though Winnicott would probably not have regarded himself primarily as a theorist, his psychoanalytic work may have significant implications for the theory of knowledge.

Let us begin with Winnicott's classic observations of infant development. In the very early period of breast-feeding, a sensitive mother may create an environment in which the infant's need for the breast coincides with his mother's provision of it, but this quickly gives way to a less comfortable world in which the wish for the breast and the reality of its provision are not synchronised. The most distinctive contribution of Winnicott is found in his description of the transitional objects that mediate between the separate worlds of desire and reality that arise at this point. Infants often use parts of their own bodies such as their fingers to substitute for the breast. Later a piece of blanket or a soft toy may be used in a similar way. Many parents instinctively understand how significant such 'transitional' objects are to children, what rich connotations they have, and how important they are to the infant's emotional equanimity. Winnicott suggests that with the creation of such objects, a transitional sphere is created that mediates between the spheres of wish and of external reality. It is a world of play and make-believe, and one that depends for its healthy development on a trusting relationship with a 'good-enough' mother. Winnicott calls it a world of 'illusory' experience, but argues that, far from being an obstacle to the perception of reality, it is a necessary step towards it. In Winnicott, there is none of Freud's hostility to 'illusion'; on the contrary it is seen as positive and healthy. It is out of this transitional sphere of play and 'illusion' that art and religion eventually develop.

It is perhaps necessary to emphasise that Winnicott is here using 'illusion' in a specialised sense. In part, his use of the term has its origins in Freud, who was careful to make a distinction between 'illusion' and the delusions of some psychiatric patients.[24] Delusions contradict reality, but illusions are not necessarily in conflict with it. When Freud called religion an 'illusion', he was making a more subtle point than the man in the street might imagine from simply seeing the title of his book. However, the positive value that Winnicott has given to 'illusion' has taken the word even further away from its everyday meaning. The gulf between the technical and everyday meanings of 'illusion' is rather similar to that which obtains for 'myth' in theology. To call aspects of religion 'illusion' no more implies that they are untrue than to call them 'myth'.

It is in this transitional world of 'illusion' that, according to psychoanalytic theorists influenced by Winnicott, the representation of God is created for the individual. In Pruyser's striking words, 'the transitional object is the transcendent'.[25] God is to be found, not wholly in the world of inner fantasy nor wholly in the world of external reality, but in the transitional world, that is, in Winnicott's terms 'outside, inside, at the border'.[26] However, the representation of God is more like a work of art than like an infant's teddy-bear. Unlike the teddy-bear, God is not gradually relegated to a psychic limbo as he is outgrown. The representation of God is rich enough to allow continual re-working and renewal. Perhaps more than any other representation in the transitional sphere, God is uniquely and power-fully related to man's sense of himself and his destiny. The world in which God is experienced is a world of 'play' and 'trust' in which man can come to understand both himself and external reality.

This Winnicottian view of religion emphasises the role of trusting human relationships in the development of religious faith. The infant's trust in the mother is in part the source of a subsequent faith in God. Nevertheless, in Meissner's words:

The assertion of faith is not merely a reassertion of basic trust ... it returns to the rudiments of trust in order to go beyond them. This faith ultimately renounces the imperfection and finitude of basic trust in order to reach beyond it and thereby to recapture it more profoundly.[27]

The creative balance between inner and outer in the transitional world is a delicate one. If there is insufficient psychic involvement, not enough 'play', meaning drains away and religious ideas lose their significance. Equally, if the religious world becomes too autistic, too merely magical, it loses its creative power. The transitional world can fall apart into mere fantasy on the one hand, and mere external ritual on the other.

There is much that is welcome in this new, Winnicottian approach to religion. It is perhaps hardly the way Freud expected his ideas would be developed when he set them out in *The Future of an Illusion*. The notion of the transitional sphere, with its integration of the inner and outer, resonates with the ideas on religion of many other thinkers. The distinction between mere fantasy and the illusional transitional world is reminiscent of the important distinction Coleridge made between fancy and imagination.[28] The concept of the transitional puts in another way what the existentialist theologian, Martin Buber, called 'the realm of the between',[29] the realm of encounter, meaning and mystery that lies between the purely objective and the purely subjective. The link of religion to other transitional activities such as art also seems likely to be fruitful, and in chapter 5 we will pursue the analogy between religious and aesthetic cognition.

Perhaps the most curious feature of the view of cognition implicit in Winnicott's work is not the introduction of a transitional sphere where inner and outer mingle, but the implicit retention of worlds of pure external reality and pure fantasy. The perception of the world is not a passive process like an image registering on a photographic film. It is something in which we are always actively and to some extent creatively engaged, even in the perception of apparently neutral and uninteresting physical features. Equally, fantasy takes reality as its raw material; images are in many ways like perceptions. So the mixing of inner and outer does not seem to be confined to what Winnicott calls the transitional sphere. The question which needs to be addressed more explicitly is exactly *how* inner and outer intertwine in the transitional sphere, and how this differs from how they intertwine in other domains. Neither psychoanalysis nor cognitive psychology have given this question the attention it deserves.

The application of Winnicott's ideas to the analysis of religion is at present rather speculative. Is it correct? Specifically, are the transitional objects of infancy really the precursors of the adult's concept of God? Winnicott himself moves perhaps too quickly from straightforward observations of transitional objects in children to more general discussion of transitional phenomena in adults. The closeness of the parallel and the postulated developmental linkage are matters that require more empirical investigation than they have yet received. Rizutto has made a valuable preliminary contribution in presenting four rich and detailed case studies relating people's psychic histories to their concepts of God.[30] However, much more empirical investigation will be required before finally accepting a Winnicottian view of religion.

Also, if God inhabits the transitional sphere, what is his status? Rizutto, like Jung, has studied the *representation* of God; but what of God himself? Is God discovered or created? Perhaps we can do no more than note that for contemporary psychoanalysts of religion, as for Jung, this is a difficult and unresolved question.

The psychoanalytic approach has led us to an emphasis on the intermingling of inner and outer, and the need to transcend it. In the next chapter we will examine the related dichotomy between faith and knowledge which has dominated philosophical theology for centuries, and conclude that it too needs to be transcended. Religious cognition, we will argue, inhabits an intermediate sphere.

# 4

## Faith and knowledge

Of the various aspects of religion that can be approached from a psychological perspective, it is with religious *knowing* that we are concerned in this book, i.e. with how people acquire knowledge of the things of God. We shall argue that there are essential similarities between religious knowing and other everyday forms of knowing. However, it is to some extent controversial whether there can be religious knowledge at all, and debate about this has generated very extensive discussion in philosophical theology. In this chapter, we will attempt to place our psychological approach to religious knowing within the context of this philosophical debate. Those who wish for a fuller discussion of the philosophical and theological issues can find it elsewhere.[1] In particular John Hick[2] and James Kellenberger[3] have approached them in a way with which we are broadly in sympathy. Our discussion of the philosophical literature here will only focus on those aspects which are relevant to the psychological purposes of this book.

So many issues about the possibility of knowing God can be traced back to the position taken up by Aquinas that it will be useful to begin with him. However, care is needed not to take him out of context. He was writing in an age of faith in which the existence of God was not in doubt. His arguments therefore had a different force in his own time from that which they appear to have if transferred to our own.[4]

In debates on this issue in his time, there was uncertainty about the relative roles to be given to *reason* and to *faith*. It was part of Aquinas' purpose to harmonise faith and reason and to argue that, though faith went beyond reason, it was consistent with reason and supported by it. One solution to the relationship between reason and faith that was in widespread circulation at the time of Aquinas, though it had been condemned by Church Councils, was the doctrine of 'double truth'. 'Solution' is perhaps too strong a word, because this doctrine simply accepted that rational intellect and religious faith would often reach different conclusions, and proposed that they should be allowed to coexist. Aquinas sought a more subtle reconciliation.

He was clearly unhappy with the idea that reason had no role in the way man approached religious faith, and sought to show how reason could underpin faith. Yet he did not believe that faith could be buttressed entirely by reason. For Aquinas, the premises of theology were based on revelation, making argument from authority the most appropriate form of argument for religious belief. 'Faith' was voluntarily choosing to accept certain beliefs on the authority of the Church. The use of 'reason', of logical arguments for the existence of God, was a subsidiary one. It was to support faith by making apparent some of its implications, and to show that faith was at least consistent with reason. Thus, Aquinas gave primacy to faith and to the teaching of the Church. Reason served a supporting role. Aquinas deployed rational arguments for the existence of God, such as arguments for a 'prime mover',[5] but there were many aspects of the Christian faith, such as the Trinity, that he considered could not be supported by such arguments. There were thus many aspects of religious faith that could not be directly vindicated by logic.

He was equally cautious in his use of logical argument to elaborate a rationally based knowledge of God. His conclusions, like those of ordinary knowledge, took propositional form. However, they had the status of knowledge, not on the strength of how they were acquired by man, but because the conclusions were known by God. Aquinas took the view that man 'cannot know what God is, but only what he is not'. His method was essentially to discern what would be incompatible with our concept of God and to elaborate the converse.[6]

The heritage we have from Aquinas' approach to these questions has a very different force in an age in which faith can no longer be assumed. When there is little faith left to be buttressed by reason, what place do Aquinas' rational arguments have? One possible response to this situation is to allow the rational case for religious belief to stand on its own, not as a buttress for faith, but as the basis of faith. This is the enterprise on which 'natural theology' has been engaged since the enlightenment.[7] Yet, the verdict on the success of this enterprise must be a bleak one. The historical record of natural theology in leading people to religious faith can only be regarded as poor.

The demise of universal religious faith coincided with a general change in the philosophical climate. Traditional rational arguments for the existence of God came under sharp attack. For example, the British empiricist philosophers had exposed serious problems with the argument from design, i.e. that because the world exhibited intelligible order it must have been created by a divine intelligence. But the development of empiricist philosophy had a much broader thrust.

It represented a radical revision of philosophical views about the nature of knowledge and the extent to which knowledge was possible. What we could truly be said to *know* appeared to be very limited. In the long run, the general approach to the theory of knowledge taken by empiricist philosophers has probably been more important to the concept of religious knowledge than their attempts to refute particular philosophical arguments for the existence of God.

In this situation, there has been an attack on the possibility of knowing God from two directions. Some philosophers have argued that it is radically mistaken to regard religious beliefs as anything that can properly be called 'knowledge'. From the other side, some theologians and religious apologists have come to think that it is inappropriate to try to buttress faith with rational argument and that, tactically, it is an enterprise better not joined because it cannot be carried off successfully.

A common thread running through many radical objections to the very concept of religious knowledge has been a sceptical position about knowledge generally. We will now briefly consider some objections to the concept of religious knowledge. Having done so we will return to the general scepticism about knowledge out of which they grew, and make some specifically psychological points about the nature of human knowledge and the way in which it has been discussed by philosophers.

## Logical positivism

Among objections to the possibility of religious knowledge, the arguments of the logical positivists are a useful starting point because they represent a clear, albeit strident, statement from a tradition rooted in the general scepticism about knowledge of empiricist philosophy. Taking scientific statements as the exemplar of empirical propositions, the logical positivists set forward the Verification Principle, from which it followed that statements could be divided into propositions of mathematics and logic on the one hand, and empirical statements on the other. Candidates for inclusion in the latter category were judged by their ability to be (at least in principle) verified by sense experience. Those statements that fell into neither category were rejected as being neither true nor false. Logical positivist philosophers differed somewhat over how to regard such residual statements, but in England the most influential view was that of Ayer who regarded ethical statements as being simply 'emotive' or 'performative' rather than factual, while theology was dismissed as being meaningless.[8]

This position remained a strong one, and set a challenge which other philosophers, not themselves logical positivists, sought to face. In the mid 1950s, Anthony Flew, in a classic symposium paper,[9] put the challenge to his fellow philosophers 'What would have to occur or to have occurred to constitute for you a disproof of the love of, or the existence of, God?' In the same year, Richard Braithwaite, though an avowed Christian, gave an inaugural lecture,[10] in which he suggested that religious doctrines should be regarded as morally helpful stories, thus suggesting essentially that religious beliefs were ethical rather than factual.

Flew told an engaging parable to make his point that religious claims are not factual and should not be treated as knowledge. Two explorers came to a well-tended clearing in a forest. One of them believed that it must be tended by a gardener, but the other disagreed. It is the apparent claim to knowledge of the first explorer which is put forward as being like apparent claims to religious knowledge. The two explorers tried to settle their disagreement empirically. They pitched tents and kept watch for a gardener, but one never appeared. Eventually, they set up an electrified barbed-wire fence and patrolled it with bloodhounds. Whatever they did, no evidence of a gardener was obtained. Eventually, the first explorer was reduced to conceding that the gardener was invisible, was unaffected by electric fences, and gave no scent or sound to alert the hounds. Flew argues that, so reduced, the apparently factual claim that there is a gardener is shown not to be such at all. Indeed it becomes apparent that it never was. It was just an imaginative picture that the first explorer chose to adopt. The same, Flew argues, is true of the apparently factual claims of a religious person.

To philosophers, it has increasingly come to seem that logical positivism's dismissal of religious belief as meaningless involves an arbitrary and over-restrictive criterion for what can be regarded as having meaning, a development in which Wittgenstein played an influential role. However, even to philosophers who have not accepted the tenets of logical positivism, it has often seemed that religious statements are not straightforwardly factual. At very least, if they are factual statements of any kind, the facts that they contain seem not to be easily verifiable. Up to a point, religious thinkers can live with this position. There has always been a tradition in religious thinking that sees God as a mystery, whose nature cannot be wholly captured in human formulations. McPherson, in Flew's 1955 symposium, sought to reconcile logical positivists' views about the meaninglessness of religious statements with theology. He saw the challenge of the logical positivists as being to some extent a helpful one from a religious point of view, because it could reduce the emphasis on the *formulation* of religious truth.[11] Formulations, he argued, are not what is important in religion and are inevitably inadequate. McPherson's perspective is a helpful one, but the rejection of religious statements as not just inadequate, but meaningless, remains an unpalatable one for the religious person.

### *'Secular' theology: van Buren*

Another possible theological response has been to argue that there is nothing peculiar about religious statements when they are properly understood, a position taken by those such as van Buren who have sought to translate the gospel into secular terms.[12] In as far as religion makes factual claims at all, these are re-construed as statements about the ordinary world rather than a distinctively religious world, as statements about man rather than about God. (We will have more to say about attempts to demythologise the Gospel in chapter 9.)

Van Buren rejects the idea that religious language makes distinctively *religious* empirical claims because this would imply (a) marking off a certain area of experience as religious and (b) postulating a distinctively religious way of knowing. However, these implications do not necessarily follow. There is no need to link an interpretation of religious language as factual with a radical dualism that splits off a religious world from a non-religious world. An example of an alternative would be a 'double-aspect' position in which religious and non-religious *facets* of experience were seen as intertwined, and religious language was seen as making empirical reference to the religious *aspects* of reality. Similarly, perception can be described from a physiological or a psychological point of view. One can talk, in factual terms, about the psychological aspects of perception without implying that they are separate from the physiological aspects. As for van Buren's second implication, the whole thrust of this book is to show how ordinary cognitive processes are at work, in large measure, in religious knowledge. It is only when we acknowledge fully the role of ordinary cognition in religious knowing that we will begin to see clearly whether or not there is a supplementary role for a distinctively religious mode of knowing.

## Evangelical fideism

A more radical religious response to philosophical scepticism about the scope of knowledge is that originally developed by Pascal in the seventeenth century. Of course it was the scepticism of an earlier generation to which he was responding. Developments in experimental science, and the confidence in the powers of the human intellect generated by scientific humanism had already created major problems for religious faith. Was there a place for God in a mechanistic universe? Pascal's position is important as the source of a tradition of religious thought still influential today, *evangelical fideism*, that rejects the possibility of religious knowledge just as firmly as the logical positivists.[13]

Pascal saw the intellect as a faculty of fallen men and therefore corrupt. From this point of view, it was clearly inappropriate to buttress faith with rational argument. Because of the corrupt nature of the human intellect, faith, alone and unaided, must lead man to God. Exposing the limitations of the intellect was central to his purpose of exposing the corrupt and sinful state of man, and hence man's need for God. In addition, Pascal thought that to try to demonstrate the existence of God intellectually was to misunderstand the nature of God. God's way is to reveal himself. Man cannot obtain knowledge of God by his own efforts unless God chooses to disclose himself. Arguments such as these are still used by many contemporary writers.

Finally, Pascal sought to buttress faith by deploying the general arguments of the philosophical sceptics, who had argued for the elusiveness of certainty in human knowledge. He argued that many of our common sense beliefs have no cast-iron rational justification. If common sense beliefs are accepted without such justification, why should not religious beliefs not be similarly accepted? This line of argument has fared relatively well among philosophers, and contemporary philosophical statements of it are common. His goal was an explicitly evangelical one, not merely to defend religious faith against intellectual attack, but to use rational argument to bring people to faith. He switched from a defensive to an attacking position, and sought to expose the limits to what could be understood by merely intellectual enquiry.

A similar position was developed by Kierkegaard, who saw a sharp incompatibility between religious faith and knowledge. Faith involves risk and uncertainty. Knowledge is certain; hence their incompatibility. To try to buttress faith by reason is to undermine its passionate subjectivity, and to avoid the 'offence' of pure faith. It is not only that there are no reasons for faith, it would be incompatible with faith to look for such reasons, even for considerations that rendered faith probable rather than otherwise.

For Pascal and Kierkegaard, there was some minimal recognition that the *content* of faith involved factual claims, but they emphasised the differences between these and ordinary factual claims. Rather than seeking to buttress the empirical basis of religious belief, they had religious reasons for glorying in its lack of empirical basis. From a philosophical point of view, Pascal conceded more to a sceptical approach to knowledge than it was necessary or even appropriate to concede. From a religious point of view, while Kierkegaard's emphasis on the passionate personal commitment involved in the religious life was a valuable corrective to cool, rational arguments for the existence of a deity, it was itself somewhat unbalanced in seeking risk and uncertainty beyond what is necessary.

Implicit scepticism about the possibility of human knowledge of God is in fact much more widespread than at first appears, and can be found even in some of those who appear to endorse such knowledge. Though Karl Barth[14] has trenchently asserted, not only the mere possibility, but the reality of knowledge of God, it is apparent on the closer examination that this is a very odd kind of knowledge. Indeed, Barth would readily concede that the unique properties of God as an object of knowledge make knowledge of God quite unlike all other knowledge. It is the 'knowledge of faith' made possible, not by human cognition, but by God's revelation of himself. Any kind of natural knowledge which seeks to discover God from a human vantage point is, for Barth, mistaken and impossible. It may seem that in specifying the unique nature of knowledge of God in this way Barth is talking about something radically different from what is ordinarily meant by knowledge. Behind his assertions of the special reality of 'knowledge' of God, he denies the possibility of any ordinary, human knowledge of God as firmly as any fideist.

## Wittgenstein

In the twentieth century, Wittgenstein has propounded a philosophical approach to religious language that has sufficient similarities with the views of the evangelical fideists for Nielson[15] to have dubbed it 'Wittgensteinian fideism'. Though differing on many points, both from logical positivists like Ayer and evangelical fideists like Pascal, he was equally unhappy with the idea that religious knowledge is possible, or that the claims of religious people have an empirical basis. His approach to this issue displays the kind of philosophical subtlety that he often shows, and lifts objections to the concept of religious knowledge to an altogether higher level of discussion. His position is also interesting in that it is associated neither with atheism or theism. His philosophical arguments are used neither to defend or to attack religion. His personal position can perhaps best be judged from the epigrammatic jottings published posthumously as *Culture and Value* and seems to be that of a sympathetic outsider. The flavour of these personal observations is reflected in the comment that 'Religion is, as it were, the calm bottom of the sea at its deepest point, which remains calm however high the waves on the surface may be.'[16]

For Wittgenstein it was simply a mistake to puzzle about the justification of religious belief. To do so is to misunderstand its nature. However, there are several reasons why Wittgenstein's position on this (and many other matters) is difficult to grasp, chief among them being the way he often expresses himself in enigmatic hints, and the extent to which he changed his views over time. In 1930,[17] Wittgenstein took the view that discourse about God appears to consist of similes, but that we are in difficulties when we try to drop the similes and state the facts behind them. We find that 'what at first appeared to be a simile now seems to be mere nonsense'. By the 1938 *Lectures and Conversations on Aesthetics, Psychology and Religious Belief,*[18] his conclusions were less sharp. On the question of whether religious people are reasonable to hold the views they do, he is clear that they cannot be said to be reasonable, but neither does he want to say that they are *un*reasonable. He would rather take the line that statements of religious belief should not be taken as rationally defensible statements of empirical fact. If religious people imagine that their beliefs are empirical statements, they have been misled about their nature. Wittgenstein might try to expose such misunderstandings about the nature of religious beliefs, but he avoided attacking the beliefs themselves. Rather, he would recognise religious talk as being internally coherent within its own 'ground rules'. The task of the philosopher would be to understand the rules of its use.

This philosophical programme has produced some insightful philosophical work on religion. An example of this, D. Z. Phillips' book on *The Concept of Prayer*,[19] will be considered in chapter 8. The problem lies not in its positive injunction to study how religious language is used, but in its apparent embargo on considering the rational justification of religious language. It is often not clear how far this embargo is meant to be pressed. However, if pressed to its limit it seems to reach a position of absurdity where it would prohibit all rational discussion of religious claims. It is also noticeable that neither Wittgenstein nor his followers have produced compelling arguments as to why religious beliefs *should* not be taken as involving rationally justifiable factual claims. At best, it has been shown that they *need* not be taken in this way.

One of the more celebrated defences of Wittgenstein's position has been provided by Malcolm in his essay 'Is it a religious belief that God exists?'[20] He makes the proper and important distinction between belief *in* God, and belief *that* God exists. Belief *in* God seems straightforward to Malcolm, but the belief *that* there is a God he finds 'a problematic concept' because it seems to suggest that there are rational grounds for it. His solution is to try to detach the two, and argue that belief *in* God does not necessarily assume *that* God exists. The absurdity of this enterprise will be clear to most people coming to the matter with fresh minds. It is an indictment of his approach that he is forced to try to argue such an unpromising case. Of course, it can readily be accepted that religion is primarily belief *in* God; but it is hard to see how this can make sense if there is no God to believe in.

## *A psychological perspective on the philosophy of knowledge*

A common element in all these objections to the idea of religious knowledge is an idealisation of knowledge that comes from philosophical scepticism. Religious knowledge is not alone in having raised problems for philosophers. The possibility of knowledge of 'other minds' (i.e. of what other people are thinking and feeling) has raised similar issues.[21] Both sets of apparent philosophical problems have a common basis. Unrealistic criteria for knowledge are set up that do not reflect those that apply in everyday life. It is then argued that because religious knowledge does not meet these unrealistic criteria it should not be regarded as knowledge at all. This is a common feature in the positions both of those who have attacked religion from an atheistic perspective, and those who have tried to re-cast religious belief on fideist foundations.

The elusiveness of 'certainty' with respect to common sense beliefs has been the subject of much discussion by contemporary philosophers. A. J. Ayer, for example, argues that we can never be sure, with regard to propositions concerning the existence of material things, that we are not being deceived.[22] Indeed, 'being sure' implies a contradition since one could not (logically could not) complete the infinite number of empirical tests necessary to verify an empirical proposition; 'infinite' means that there is always one more that can be added to a series. But how then are we to characterise everyday examples of things about which we have no doubt – such as the fact that I am holding this pen, writing this sentence, sitting in this chair? Wittgenstein, in 'On Certainty',[23] argues that philosophers have often used the word 'know' inappropriately. To use the term 'know' in the context of such 'bedrock propositions' is misleading. Differences in the contextual appropriateness of the use of the word 'know' are important.

It is too facile to argue, as Pascal did, that many of our common sense beliefs have no cast-iron rational justification, so that religious beliefs may be accepted on the same basis as the bedrock propositions of everyday life. There are different kinds of knowledge, different language games in which 'I know' appears. Because of this, the question ought to be whether religious knowing can properly be included in the knowledge family. In practice, in assessing a particular claim to knowledge, one looks to the balance of evidence, both to evaluate how certain a proposition is, and to ascertain in what language-game it is being used.

It is in determining how far claims to knowledge correspond to 'reality' that philosophy tends to merge with psychology. Philosophers commonly select propositions such as 'I feel pain' as prototypical examples of reports of psychological states of which we can be certain, at some level, without it being possible for other people to verify. 'I feel pain' makes a psychological claim about which no one could disagree, for it makes no claim about the external, verifiable origins of the pain. On the same basis, statements such as 'I feel God's presence' or 'I know God is with me' are only unchallengeable if made as psychological statements. If, however, they are put forward as statements which imply the existence of God, then (the argument runs) one must be able to specify the public checking procedures available to bolster this existential claim. Since these public checking procedures are not available with respect to propositions about God, it is nonsense to claim 'knowledge' of him. Let us try to indicate how psychological investigation can elucidate some of the argument about 'public tests and checking procedures' as criteria of knowledge.

Firstly, psychologists have developed methods of checking hypotheses about perception, awareness, memory, etc., which can make as much use of observations of a single individual as of observations from a group of individuals. In the field of perception, for example, repeated trials in which a single subject is exposed to dim lights of carefully regulated intensities can establish a person's lower threshold for seeing light. A single subject's perceptual thresholds, and the way in which he or she varies in the confidence of making such perceptual judgements can be accurately specified. More importantly, a knowledgeable subject could do the same experiment on himself and soon gain a great deal of confidence in his or her own judgement, irrespective of what other people may or may not be able to perceive themselves in the dimly lit laboratory. It could be suggested that this procedure has involved public checks (i.e. the instruments) but it is the subject himself who has initiated the checks and determined the point at which he 'knows' whether a light is on or off. He has become the 'expert', the testimony of public witnesses notwithstanding.

There are other, more commonly experienced situations in which subjective certainty may give as good a guide to the truth of a proposition as public checks. Consider the 'tip of the tongue' phenomenon. Imagine standing in a group of people who are all struggling to remember the name of a school friend from twenty years ago. Four of them are fairly sure it was Brown, another two say they think it was Brand. Suddenly you remember it was Brinn. Even before you tell them 'Of course, it was Brinn', you *know* you're right. You know when you've 'got it' because it feels so completely different from all the near-misses with which you've been struggling. Philosophers who are selective about the 'psychological' statements they choose to use in arguments rarely take into account these complex aspects of 'subjective' knowledge.

A tendency by philosophers to select certain special types of psychological statements and to treat them as prototypical can be seen in C.B. Martin's arguments against claims by Christians to have knowledge of God.[24] One may be certain of one's experience, he says, but only if one's statements remain merely statements about one's psychology. 'Absolute confidence, and absolute indifference to the majority judgement is bought at the price of reducing the existential to the psychological.' He gives the psychological statement 'I feel pain' and shows how it loses nothing by making its psychological status explicit: 'I seem to feel pain'. Why, though, choose a pain-statement? An alternative psychological statement would have produced different conclusions. For example 'I remember that café in Germany' represents a different level of confidence from 'I seem to remember ...' Once again, the selection of only one statement ignores the subtleties of a person's subjective checking procedures and his own criteria for what is known and what is only strongly suspected.

There is one final argument used by several philosophers against those who would make an existential claim from their statement about knowledge of God. Martin again: '"I seem to be listening to a choir" has meaning only in so far as I already *know* what it is like to be listening to a choir.' Even the 'seem' statement is likely to be false if there is no such prior knowledge. Since there is nothing about experience of God which could count as knowledge, claims to know God are invalid. But Martin has assumed in this argument that which he wishes to prove – that he cannot have knowledge of God. The argument also depends on selectivity in choosing examples. Consider the alternative. 'I seem to be having a heart attack.' This statement is relatively common, reflecting a person's puzzlement about the nature of symptoms he or she is experiencing. But the subjective confusion has no bearing upon whether he or she actually is or is not having a heart attack. The existential statement underlying the subjective statement has a truth value, so 'I seem to be having a heart attack' does indeed have meaning even though I do not have prior knowledge of what it is like to have a heart attack.

These examples serve as reminders that in discussing the status of our knowledge statements we need to take account of empirical psychological factors, whether one is discussing religious or nonreligious propositions.

Just as psychological and philosophical approaches to knowledge have different emphases, so do psychological and philosophical approaches to the basis of religious belief. The philosopher sees rational argument as being, in principle, convincing. Indubitable premises are sought, valid arguments are employed, and correct conclusions reached. Anyone intellectually capable of following the argument should be persuaded of the truth of the conclusions. Of course, there is often fierce debate about whether or not particular arguments are valid, but the arguments are nevertheless *intended* to be universally convincing. The classical philosophical arguments for the existence of God are of this kind.

Psychologists, in contrast, are concerned with the empirical nature of religious belief and its bases, rather than with an abstract analysis of what in principle it might be based on. Our proposal is that faith is 'cognitive', a proposal which is different in important ways from the related philosophical issue of whether faith is rationally justifiable.

Psychologists are keenly aware that it is very common in everyday life for human cognitive processes to lead to incorrect conclusions; indeed it is characteristic of human cognition that it proceeds in a way that allows for this possibility. When people try to grasp what is happening in a particular situation they generally use heuristic strategies ('rules of thumb') to interpret the information available to them. Good heuristics are those that lead to correct conclusions most of the time, on the basis of whatever information is available and do so as rapidly and efficiently as possible. It is not in the nature of every-day human cognition for people to suspend judgement until they are logically justified in reaching a particular conclusion.

The implication of this for present purposes is that the claim that religious understanding is cognitive is a much more limited one than the claim discussed by philosophers of whether it is rationally justifiable.[25] The former is simply a claim that there is some com-monality between the cognitive processes by which certain people arrive at religious conclusions and those by which all of us arrive at everyday conclusions about experience. In this book we try to specify these commonalities.

## Similarities between scientific and religious knowledge

Among those philosophers who have argued that religious knowledge is possible, and that it has an empirical basis, most have drawn an analogy between scientific and religious knowledge.[26] In the course of discussions of this analogy between science and religion, many good points have been made about the way in which religious belief can relate to evidence, though in the end we will conclude that, of the many examples available of how beliefs can be based on evidence, science is not the closest to religion. In fact, the emphasis on science in recent philosophy of religion probably owes little to the actual closeness of the analogy between scientific and religious knowledge. It probably arises partly from a survival of the positivist idea that science represents a paradigmatic form of empirical knowledge, and partly from the excitement generated by the more flexible and realistic approaches to scientific method that philosophers have developed recently. In particular, there has been a recognition that the relation-ship between experimental evidence and scientific hypotheses is more subtle and less direct than used to be assumed.

'All scientific data are theory-laden' has been one of the slogans (coined by Hanson)[27] of the new philosophy of science. Data do not come in the neutral a-theoretical form on which an unbiased choice between theories can be based. Another point that has been made prominently by Kuhn[28] is that scientific enquiry tends to be con-ducted within the framework of a 'paradigm' that embodies a set of conceptual, methodological and metaphysical assumptions. The extent to which data falsifies a paradigm is limited. A change of paradigm, Kuhn has argued, is not a direct response to logic and evidence, but needs to be understood in sociological as well as empirical terms.

In this new climate, some philosophers of religion began to suggest that the relation between empirical evidence and religious hypotheses was rather similar to that which obtained for scientific hypotheses. Religious experience, like scientific data, comes not in a raw form, but already interpreted in the light of theoretical or doctrinal concepts. Similarly, the religious paradigm, like large-scale scientific ones, is not easily open to falsification. Evidence may be relevant, but in a way that is no more direct than the role of evidence in leading to a paradigm change in science. Kuhn himself has made the point that paradigm shifts in science are in some ways like religious conversions.

This line of argument has some attractions. It suggests how it may be possible to tread a careful line between making theism rest directly and straightforwardly on empirical evidence and making it so unrelated to evidence as to be completely arbitrary and irrational. With both scientific paradigms and theism it can be argued that evidence has an indirect and cumulative role. Basil Mitchell in *The Justification of Religious Belief*[29] deploys just this argument, but adds that scientific paradigms are not the only cases where evidence is brought to bear indirectly and cumulatively. Evidence can also operate cumulatively in other fields such as history and critical exegesis. This is helpful because the analogy between theism and scientific paradigms cannot be pressed too far. Theism appears to be even less directly related to evidence than are scientific paradigms, but on the other hand to have greater power to capture the imagination and guide behaviour.

Although seeing religious thought as a scientific paradigm is attractive, it seems to misrepresent it in some ways. It is significant that theism has generally only been said to be *like* a scientific paradigm, not to *be* one. Whatever the potential of the analogy it is surely clear that religious ideas are not just hypotheses. Saints, prophets and mystics have not entertained them in the manner in which hypotheses are entertained, with argument and evidence carefully considered. On the contrary, they have clearly felt that they *knew* God in a direct and immediate way. The directness and immediacy that often characterises knowledge of God, especially at times of religious conversion, seems to have no parallels in how scientific hypotheses are arrived at.

The ideas of Ian Ramsey[30] seem to offer a partial resolution, within the framework of the scientific analogy, of this apparent disjunction between the directness of religious knowledge, and the more considered, propositional nature of scientific knowledge. He took as his starting point the way in which 'models' are employed in current philosophy of science. As we have seen, it has been recognised that in trying to conceptualise and understand new phenomena, scientists often use analogies between new phenomena and something more familiar. As these analogies are developed, a full-scale 'analogical model' of the phenomenon can be formulated. The relationship that such models are presumed to have to reality is a subtle one. They are not to be taken as literally true, but neither are they treated as mere useful fictions. Ramsey has suggested that Christians make use of similar analogical models, such as the use of human fatherhood as a model for God. It seems that neither scientific models nor religious analogies are just useful fictions. They are taken seriously as a pointer to the truth, though they are not accepted as literally true. However, this assumed similarity between religious and scientific 'analogical' thinking clearly cannot be pressed too far before it breaks down.

The key point here relates to the kind of experiences that sometimes characterise the discovery of such models. Ramsey is impressed by how, in a moment of insight, previously puzzling phenomena suddenly fall into a comprehensible pattern, and he renamed 'analogue' models as 'disclosure' models to capture this aspect of them. Thus, for Ramsey, when a Christian grasps the father model of God, the fatherhood nature of God is 'disclosed' to him. This gives some assistance in bridging the gap between scientific understanding and religious experience though it perhaps exaggerates the frequency with which the scientist, in developing an analogical model, feels that truth has been disclosed. Even when this happens, such scientific disclosure doesn't have the same power to arouse feeling and commitment as religious experience.

Philosophical discussion of the analogy between scientific and religious knowledge has been of value in indicating how religious beliefs, despite their indirect relation to evidence, can be regarded as knowledge. However, it is far from clear that science provides the best analogy for religious knowledge. There may be other examples of human cognition that are more similar to religious insight than the scientist making a discovery. It is one of the important contributions that psychology can make that it provides an extensive and detailed map of human cognition. Armed with such a map it may be possible to find better analogues of religious insight. This is a point that

James Kellenberger has made well in *Religious Discovery, Faith and Knowledge*.[31] One of his examples is the man who discovers that he is jealous of his own son. Such personal insights seem better than scientific ones as an analogue of religious insight in several respects. Their relation to empirical reality is more similar; both personal and religious insights are taken seriously as true, but they are not arrived at as a result of the detached, explicit search for discovery that characterises science. Also, they can have a degree of emotional impact and life-changing power that far exceed scientific insights and again make them closer to religious insight. The arena where personal insights have been observed most closely is in psychotherapy. When, in the next chapter we examine analogues of religious knowing, we will suggest that one of the best available ones is the way people arrive at insights about themselves in psychotherapy.

## Beyond rationalism and fideism

The traditional debate between those who believe that religious knowledge is rationally justifiable and those who believe that religion can only be based on a kind of faith that is wholly distinct from reason, has left little room for a third possibility to be discussed. The debate has too often been one of faith *or* reason. We suggest that it is both unnecessary and unfortunate that it has often been presented in these polarised terms.

Firstly, it is a dichotomy which cognitive psychology has shown to be misleading. We have indicated already how general philosophical scepticism, which is the bedrock of many objections to religious knowledge, arises from concentration on highly selected examples. Equally, the sharp cleavage between rational demonstration and voluntary faith that is assumed in much discussion on the basis of religious belief from Aquinas to the present day does violence to the actual nature of cognitive processes. It fails to recognise how what we perceive is inextricably intertwined with our assumptions, hypotheses and preoccupations. The point here is very similar to the one we have already noted in recent philosophy of science about data being 'theory-laden'.

One of the most commonly cited examples of the way in which the mind constructs reality out of raw perception is the Necker Cube. This two-dimensional array of lines (shown in the figure) is almost impossible to perceive except as a three-dimensional cube. However, one may notice more about the Necker Cube than that two dimensions are perceived as three. Firstly it appears that the mind 'creates an

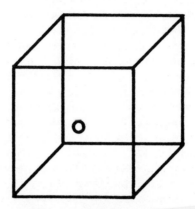

Figure 1.　The Necker Cube.

The figure alternates in depth: the face of the cube marked
by the small circle sometimes appearing as the *front*,
sometimes as the *back* face. We can think of these ways
of seeing the figure as perceptual 'hypotheses'.

hypothesis' about how to perceive the cube, and that, after a while,
the brain tries an alternative hypothesis. If one studies the cube, it
tends to reverse spontaneously and what was the back wall of the cube
appears now to be the front wall. Secondly, it appears that the mind
does not entertain two hypotheses at the same time. What is perceived at any one moment is the product of (a) certain stimulus elements
and (b) the current 'hypothesis' about how the elements cohere.[32]
The perception of the meanings of words proceeds in very much the
same way. When a word is read, or heard, the mind sets up hypotheses
about subsequent words − it makes a bet on which words are coming
next. This effect can be demonstrated by examining the speed with
which someone can identify a word (such as butter) if they have just
read an associate (bread) or an irrelevant word (tree). People are much
quicker to recognise 'butter' if 'bread' has recently been presented to
them; it is as if the brain has made the prediction and needs very little
confirmation.

Both these examples reflect how people's expectations, previous
experience and assumptions intertwine with raw experience to produce
what is actually perceived. In addition, the preoccupations of particular individuals influence what they perceive. A good example
comes from homophones, two words with quite distinct meanings that
sound almost identical (e.g. weak, week; ail, ale). When people hear

homophones in isolation, they are inclined to 'hear' the word that is congruent with their emotional preoccupations.

People thus actually perceive the world in the image of their assumptions about what it is like. There is thus likely to be no sharp cleavage in religious perception between 'faith' (i.e. assumptions about the religious basis of the world) and 'knowledge' (i.e. the empirical basis on which religious beliefs can rationally be based). The two reach human experience already intertwined

In his recent book on *The Cognitivity of Religion*,[33] James Kellenberger has also argued for seeing beyond the over-simple dichotomy presented by faith and reason. He presents what he calls a 'third perspective' which can mediate between the more extreme views of the rationalists and the fideists who have tended to dominate debate on the basis of religious belief. Kellenberger presents this third view as being based on the *discovery* of God. The analogue of a father discovering that he is jealous of his own son, to which we have already referred, indicates the kind of discovery process he has in mind. However, he also emphasises that the 'cognitive' or 'discovery' perspective has a long tradition in Judeo-Christian thought, and cites the Psalms as a place where it can be found most clearly. Kellenberger suggests that the psalmist sees evidence of God all around him. However, it is not the neutral evidence of rational argument or scientific data, but the evidence that is available *if* the world is seen as a God-filled place. It is not evidence that stares everyone in the face, but it is available only to those who 'open their hearts' and see it. Kellenberger traces this discovery tradition through a number of Christian writers. It is in the contemplatives and mystics of the Church that it can be found most clearly, for example in the Franciscan mystic, Bonaventura, who urges 'open your eyes ... prick up your spiritual ears, open your lips, and apply your heart, that you may see your God in all creatures'.[34]

Having traced the discovery perspective through religious writings, Kellenberger then compares it with rationalism and fideism on several key controversies regarding the basis of religious belief. On the question of whether religion is 'cognitive at its core', the discovery perspective joins the rationalists in saying that it is. However, the discovery perspective would share many of the objections voiced by fideists about the way in which the cognitive aspect of religion has been presented in the rationalist tradition. Discovering God is not merely assenting to a metaphysical theory. A process of personal transformation is necessarily involved in discovering God. Similarly, the discovery perspective recognises, with the rationalists, that there *can*

be evidence for belief in God, but would share the fideists' objections
to the relevance of the kind of *enquiry*-evidence that the rationalists
are concerned with. On the central question of whether there can
be religious knowledge, the discovery perspective would side with
rationalists in asserting that there *can* be fully fledged knowledge
claims. Discovering God brings one to a kind of knowledge. It
would thus make no sense to deny the possibility of knowledge of
God, though the discovery perspective would again share the fideists'
suspicion of the *kind* of knowledge of God that the rationalists have
sought.

Both rationalism and fideism share restrictive assumptions about
the nature of human knowledge, assumptions which have unfortunate
consequences that extend beyond the territory of philosophical
theology. There has been a widespread failure, not just in religious
circles, to understand that there can be personal knowledge, a
knowledge of the heart, knowledge into which imagination enters.
There have, of course, been notable exceptions to this widespread
neglect. Winnicott's 'transitional' sphere, that we discussed in the last
chapter, is a place where this kind of imaginative thinking can be
located. Michael Polanyi's *Personal Knowledge*[35] has become a
classic, and is particularly valuable for the way in which it draws
attention to the role of personal participation in scientific work.
Martin Heidegger's view of thinking also contains an emphasis on the
thinking of the heart. For example, he traces the word 'thought' to
the Old English noun 'thane', which means a grateful thought,
and 'memory' to its earlier meaning of devotion and thoughtful
meditation.[36] Such thinkers, outside the religious domain, have
sought to argue the case for a kind of knowledge which is personal and
requires emotional involvement, but nevertheless has the objectivity
that justifies it being called knowledge. They have described a kind of
knowledge that is *subjective* in the sense of being personal, but also
*objective* in that it is concerned with the truth about things, but have
seen no contradiction between the two. We suggest that it is this kind
of knowing that is the basis of religious belief.

The New Testament has a concept of insightful perception which
appears to stand somewhere between ordinary perception and faith.
For example, an analysis of the various words for 'see' used in St
John's gospel[37] has disclosed an implicit hierarchical scheme starting
from mere registration of a visual image, and moving through looking
at something with concentration and fascination, to seeing with
intuitive understanding, and finally to seeing in the sense that occurs
between people in a loving encounter. It has been suggested that faith

(used in St John's gospel in its verbal form) represents a final extension of this hierarchical development of ways of seeing.

Among theologians, Aquinas described 'knowledge by connaturality', which he saw as the basis of contemplative knowledge of God.[38] Contemplation involves the union of knower and object, of the contemplative and God, in love and mutual indwelling. It is a knowledge of acquaintance, corresponding to that of the lover and the loved, though it necessarily also implies an enrichment of understanding. This kind of contemplative knowledge of God, of which there is a rich and varied tradition, suggests the possibility of direct religious knowing.

In this century there have been several influential figures who have argued, not only that it is *possible* to transcend the dichotomy between rationalism and fideism, but that it is *important* from many points of view that this should be done. The French Islamic scholar, Corbin has urged that mediating between what he calls 'believing' and 'knowing' there is the third possibility of 'inner vision' which operates in an 'intermediate and mediating world forgotten by the official philosophy of our times, the *mundus imaginatis*, the imaginal world'.[39] In similar vein, Jung has expressed concern about the cleavage between faith and knowledge and suggested it represents a collective psychological disturbance. After commenting on the curious way in which 'archaic rites and conceptions' of denominational religion survive in a predominantly scientific culture, he says:

The rupture between faith and knowledge is a sympton of the *split consciousness* which is so characteristic of the mental disorder of our day. It is as if two different persons were making statements about the same thing, each from his own point of view, or as if one person in two different frames of mind were sketching a picture of his experience. If for 'person' we substitute 'modern society', it is evident that the latter is suffering from a mental dissociation, i.e. a neurotic disturbance.[40]

Rudolf Steiner[41] has also expressed concern about the significance of the sharp dichotomy between faith and reason which he believes can be traced back to Aquinas. Steiner argues that Aquinas paved the way for the view that Pascal expressed more polemically, that reason is a faculty of fallen man that is thereby limited in its capacity to attain the highest truths. However, it seemed to Steiner that a Christian cannot rest content with the view that knowledge is corrupt and beyond redemption. If human cognition is 'fallen', Steiner argued, the Christian hope must be that it will be redeemed. Such redemption of human cognition would involve its transformation into something that is capable of the apprehension of God. For Steiner, the question that has not been answered satisfactorily is 'How does Christ enter into human thinking?' His own answer is that there is a need to develop a new kind of thinking that is living, imaginative and Christ-filled.

The consequences of this would be felt on a broad front. It would not only make genuine religious knowing increasingly possible, but, Steiner argued, also transform natural and social science. Developing Steiner's position, Charles Davy has argued that it would make possible a third culture, based on imaginative but objective thinking, that transcended the sciences and the humanities.[42] We share Steiner's view that the issues raised by direct religious knowing do not apply solely to religion. Religious knowing is not *sui generis*. The cognitive capacities needed for experimental religious knowing can be found in other fields of human cognition. Equally, any extension of the capacity for religious knowing will have consequences for cognition in other domains. It is to tracing similarities between direct religious knowing and other forms of cognition that we will now turn.

In this chapter it has been possible to do no more than sketch out some of the vast and complex literature in philosophical theology that is the background to our own programme of describing the cognitive processes in religious understanding. It has inevitably been a selective sketch in which we have identified sympathetic voices and at least hinted at why we are not persuaded by some apparently unsympathetic ones. Our central thrust has been to reject the common assumption that religious beliefs are arrived at by a process of 'faith' that is wholly distinct from the cognitive processes by which other human knowledge is acquired.

# 5

## Analogues of religious knowing

There are some obvious objections that can be raised to the proposition that the cognitive processes that enter into the religious interpretation of experience are similar to those that operate in other contexts. Why, if this is so, is religious experience so idiosyncratic and unpredictable? If I go to an arboretum with a group of normal adults I can be confident that they will *all* see trees there, and come away knowing that they have seen trees. Now religious experience is clearly not like this. Whether it occurs in an explicitly religious context or not (and for many of David Hay's respondents referred to in chapter 2, it did not), such experience is either rare, or so weak and uncertain that it leaves people unsure about exactly what sort of phenomenon they have experienced. If religious experience is so unusual and uncertain, how can we claim that it is based on everyday cognitive processes?

In the last chapter, we referred to psychotherapeutic insight as a useful analogue of a sort of 'knowing' which consists neither of simply intellectual propositions nor simply of emotional feelings. In this chapter we wish to explore this 'knowing' in greater depth by examining other domains in which similar processes appear to be operating. Specifically we shall suggest that there are certain elements that psychotherapeutic insight shares with aesthetics and with empathy: they involve a clarity of perception; this clarity may be enhanced by meditation; and the perception itself may have implications for subsequent behaviour. Our purpose in examining these elements is to see how far each may be related to religious knowing and to consider how findings from a range of psychological studies can illuminate the type of 'perception' that is involved. Finally, we return to psychotherapeutic insight and examine again the extent to which it is analogous to religious knowing.

## Aesthetic 'knowing'

It ought to be conceded at the outset of a discussion of the similarity between the cognitive processes involved in aesthetic and religious sensitivity that psychological research on aesthetics has not been as productive as one could wish.[1] Much experimental work has employed such impoverished materials, artificially constructed for research purposes and sometimes not even intended to have any artistic merit, that it is doubtful whether it is of much relevance at all to understanding aesthetic sensitivity. It has also been much concerned with hedonic responses to artistic materials, or with judgements of preference or evaluation, rather than with aesthetic *cognition*. We will therefore have to rely largely on non-technical accounts, such as that of Harold Osborne in *The Art of Appreciation*[2] and the excellent essay by the psychologist, Jerome Bruner.[3]

Though there is no exact consensus on the nature of aesthetic cognition, one widely accepted tenet is that it involves a kind of distancing. Bullough, the primary source of this doctrine, puts it like this. In aesthetic perception, we separate the object from ourself. We put it 'out of gear with our practical, actual self; by allowing it to stand outside the context of our personal needs and ends − in short, by looking at it "objectively"'. In this way, the contemplation of the object alone becomes possible.[4]

This contemplation of the object of art requires a degree of intellectual restraint. Discursive thought *about* it has to be suspended if we are to be able to *see* the object properly. It is also necessary to stop thinking about past or future preoccupations, and to be centred in the present; and to 'reach out' to the work of art, rather than becoming absorbed with our own reaction to it.

This contemplative absorption needs to be in some degree an emotional one. Feelings of affection and reverence are necessarily involved. Without them, all that is possible is a critical analysis of the work of art, not aesthetic perception of it.

However, emotional restraint is also required. Bruner brings this out clearly in his account of the cognitive processes in aesthetic knowing. Seeing a work of art may set various emotional impulses in train. He describes how looking at the statue of the half-smiling Virgin in Toledo Cathedral may arouse impulses 'to father her, be mothered by her, make love to her, gossip with her, and just to watch how the face will change when the Child finally pokes her under the chin'.[5] However, impulses at the centre of consciousness have to be restrained if the web of associations at the fringes of consciousness are to elaborate themselves. There also has to be restraint of any direct striving for results while viewing the work of art, and restraint of too much involvement, else 'in place of the experience of art there is either a daydream or merely action'.

The ability to perceive art in this way is by no means universal. It is a specialised perceptual skill that some people acquire more easily than others. Even when the general skill has been acquired, it cannot invariably be brought into operation. There are times when we are too tired or preoccupied to respond to art in this way. Usually repeated attention is necessary before a work of art is properly seen. The moment when this occurs, though somewhat unpredictable, can be sudden and dramatic:

When a work of art is successfully apprehended in appreciation the new aesthetic object which is actualised to awareness is perceived with more lucidity, as if a caul had been removed from in front of it. It is sharper and more vivid in detail as if it had been removed from the periphery to the focus of vision and it acquires a structure by which it is compacted into a unified configuration.[6]

In all these ways, it seems that aesthetic cognition is a relatively good analogue of religious cognition. The religious person needs to acquire a steady contemplation of the divine that is in some ways like the aesthetic contemplation of a work of art. This is very different from discursive theological thought. The religious person also needs to put self-preoccupation aside. Further, the kind of contemplation of God which is cultivated in prayer, because it is sustained by love of God, is necessarily an emotional response. Efforts to contemplate God are sometimes rewarded only with the experience of 'aridity' that contemplatives over the centuries have described so vividly and bitterly. However, with repetition and persistence, moments of illumination are reported to follow in which the caul is removed, and God is discerned with a directness and certainty that is like the moment when the work of art is suddenly 'seen'.

Despite these similarities, there are some differences. Religious cognition seems to be less 'elitist' than aesthetic cognition. There are also differences in the extent to which religious knowing carries moral and behavioural commitments (though the two sorts of cognition may not be so dissimilar as they at first seem, a point to which we will return in discussing another 'analogue' later in this chapter). There is a further difference in the nature of what is contemplated. Though 'seeing' a picture in a fully aesthetic sense is an unusual skill, everyone can in some sense at least see *that* there is a picture, and roughly what colours and shapes it contains. It seems that religious cognition may be different in that whereas the religious contemplative claims to discern God, the non-religious person discerns nothing religious at all.

However, even this apparent difference may not be as sharp as originally appears. Osborne insists that once we have really 'seen' an object of art, we are seeing something new and different. It is, in a sense, misleading to say that we are still looking at the same thing. In religious cognition, the raw experience of life which forms the basis of contemplation is of course common to everyone in somewhat the same way as a painting is a common property of everyone. However, once the presence of God has been discerned in experience, the religious person is seeing something different in a sense that is not wholly dissimilar to that in which aesthetic perception results in seeing a new and different object of art.

Of modern religious writers, Simone Weil has probably been most explicit in writing about the powers of attention involved in the love of God. Though she does not explicitly draw the parallel with aesthetic perception, her account of religious attention is wholly consistent with the view we are developing here. In fact, her most explicit account of religious attention is developed in the context of a different, rather surprising 'analogue' in her celebrated essay on 'the right use of academic studies with a view to the love of God'.[7] She suggests that a quality of openness is a key part of the quality of attention that underlies both academic study and the love of God. 'Attention consists of suspending our thought, leaving it detached, empty and ready to be penetrated by the object ... all wrong translations, all absurdities in geometry problems, all clumsiness of style and all faulty connection of ideas in compositions and essays, all such things are due to the fact that thought has seized upon some idea too hastily and being thus prematurely blocked, is not open to the truth. The cause is always that we have wanted to be too active, ... for all academic study there is a special way of waiting upon truth, setting our hearts upon it, yet not allowing ourselves to go out in search of it.'

In the same essay Simone Weil also discusses the role of 'attention' in the 'love of our neighbour'. She draws a connection between the sort of perception and attention involved in studying with that involved in perceiving others. Indeed there are many similarities between aesthetic and empathic knowing.

## Empathic knowing

Etymologically, the connection between aesthetic and empathic cognition is a direct one, as the term 'empathy' (or rather, the German 'Einfühlung' of which it is the English equivalent) was originally introduced to describe aesthetic perception, though it has come to be used almost exclusively in the context of person perception. Like the other analogues of religious cognition discussed in this chapter, empathy involves a specialised perceptual skill that requires patient cultivation and works somewhat unpredictably. However, there are two particular aspects of empathic cognition which it is relevant to emphasise. One concerns the role of emotion, the other the 'non-analytical' nature of the cognitive processes involved in empathy. In order to understand how this is the case, we need to examine the psychotherapeutic literature which has studied empathy as a therapeutic skill.

It is part of the classical concept of empathy that it involves vicarious emotional experience.[8] Sharing the emotions of another person, and seeing things from their point of view, are two intertwined aspects of empathy that facilitate each other. Like many of the analogues discussed in this chapter, psychological research has taken only limited steps to understanding the nature of empathy but the distinctions which have emerged, and the particular way in which they combine do reveal something of the complexity of the concept.

It has been proposed that there are two alternative modes of perceiving other people, the analytical and the non-analytical.[9] Empathy involves the latter, and is thus a form of intuitive cognition. A considerable body of research on individual differences in person perception has endeavoured to develop tests that would measure capacities for analytical and non-analytical person perception. For example, in one such task an individual is given some information about another person and is then asked to predict how they would behave in certain situations. This 'behavioural prediction task' was designed to assess non-analytical person perception, though there is now some doubt about whether it actually does measure this. However, there are other more recently developed tests measuring sensitivity to implied meanings and non-verbal cues that seem to capture the concept of non-analytical empathic cognition rather better. The evidence suggests that when reacting intuitively, people use cues that they are not aware of having used, and which differ from those that they would use when operating more consciously and rationally.

This intuitive or empathic listening has been called 'Listening with the third ear'.[10] Freud recommended that analysts listen to their patients with a kind of 'evenly suspended attention' in which they avoid selecting out what seems important in what patients say and attaching particular significance to it. To search too hard for meaning and interpretation he saw as a potential source of error. Though there is some doubt about the extent to which psychotherapists actually practice this style of listening, it seems that it is at least possible for them to listen to patients in this non-analytical way. Perhaps the main rationale for it is that the significance of what patients say is often not immediately clear, with the result that any immediate interpretations are likely to be to some extent arbitrary. The similarity between the advice of Freud to would-be therapists, and of Weil to would-be students about not too hastily seizing upon an idea is striking indeed. It is interesting to consider that if a psychotherapist were to take Freud's advice, he would in fact be cultivating a conscious style of 'not knowing'.[11] We shall return to this later in discussing religious knowing.

## Meditation and perception

In both the study of aesthetics and of empathy, it has become clear that a certain perceptual style is involved. We have seen how various authors have used different terms to describe this quality of non-judgemental perception of objects or persons: 'looking objectively'; 'contemplative absorption'; 'suspending thought'; 'nonanalytic person perception'; 'intuitive listening'; 'listening with the third ear'; 'evenly suspended attention'. Can psychological theory or research throw any more light on what these authors are trying to describe? Particularly helpful here is research on how meditation affects the ordinary processes of perception.

The most careful research to have been conducted on meditation on an external physical object is that of Arthur Deikman.[12] The subjects, who had no background of mystical experience, came to a series of 12 sessions, each conducted in a quiet, subdued room, in which the central object was a blue vase. They each sat in a comfortable armchair, and were told that they had to concentrate on the vase, not thinking about it, but just seeing it 'as it exists in itself', and to exclude all other thoughts and sensations. Each session was followed by a tape-recorded enquiry in which the subjects described their experiences.

All the subjects reported some unusual perceptual phenomena. The shape of the vase became unstable, and its colour became more intense, vivid and luminous. On occasions subjects reported other experiences, such as that they felt they were merging with the vase and that the vase was radiating heat towards them. Time seemed to pass very quickly, they became very absorbed in the session and increasingly untroubled by noises around them. The participants had some difficulties in reporting their experiences, and descriptions were quite often internally conflicting, e.g. that the vase did, but also did not, fill the visual field. Though it is likely that these experiences were genuine, it must be noted that all the subjects were personally known to Deikman, and that he conducted the enquiry at the end of each session himself. The possibility of some unintentional influence over their reports cannot be ruled out.

Deikman considered that in this simple setting, using untrained subjects, he had produced at least a partial analogue of mystical experience (though his comparison of his subjects' reports of their experiences with passages from *The Cloud of Unknowing* is perhaps rather extreme). A more relevant comparison would be the traditional exercises of concentrative meditation, especially those such as the Tibetan exercises that make common use of visually perceived objects.

It is important at this point to emphasise how perceptual processes normally operate, that perception is an *active* process in which we select and organise the available information about the world to arrive at our experience of it. This 'construction' of the world out of our raw sensory input normally proceeds automatically and without awareness. Deikman explains the perceptual phenomena reported by his subjects in terms of 'de-automisation' by which is meant re-investing actions and perceptions that normally proceed automatically with deliberate attention. He proposes a fundamental dichotomy between two 'modes' of perceiving the world, an active and a receptive one. The kind of perception induced by meditation he regards as an example of the latter. The effect of meditation may be to induce a suspension of the stages of perception in which people synthesise a representation of the object before them.

This view has received its most elaborate formulation from Brown[13] in his exposition of the stages through which visual perception develops in Buddhist Yoga. One of the earlier stages of concentrative meditation is an apparent separation of cognitive from perceptual content. The meditator is left with pure perceptual content consisting of mere 'signs'. If he is meditating on a stone he is aware of roundness and brightness, but the object itself becomes insubstantial and loses the obvious solidity and durability that it has in normal perception. The disintegration of normal perception goes further, until only a point remains. Later, even this point is dissolved and only 'subtle cognitions' remain in which the meditator is directly aware of the perceptual and cognitive phenomena that are normally united in 'gross cognition'. The suggestion that what is being described here is a progressive abandonment of normal constructive processes in perception has a good deal of plausibility.

Also relevant here is the distinction between tacit and articulate modes of cognition.[14] A simple example would be scanning for some particular object, perhaps scanning a newspaper for certain names. To do this, it is not necessary to become explicitly aware of each word that is scanned. Indeed it is a good deal more efficient to scan the words without doing so, i.e. tacitly. It is a skill that needs to be learned. People who work as newspaper scanners seem to need to learn *not* to construct a representation of the words at an articulate level, but to respond directly to the information in the optical array. Halwes[14] sees an analogy between this skill and the style of perception that is learned in Buddhist meditation. Tacit cognition, apart from being faster and more efficient, may also be qualitatively different from articulate perception. It may make distinctions that we don't normally make consciously and not make distinctions that we normally do make. In particular it may be less restricted than articulate cognition and enable us to become aware of things of which we have no prior experience.

The constructivist view of perception, on which we have largely relied in the argument so far, has not gone unchallenged. Though there is agreement that perception is not a purely passive process, there is some disagreement about whether it is appropriate to break perception down into the registration of basic sensory information and a subsequent act of synthesis. Against this some psychologists, notably James Gibson, have argued that there is a direct relationship between external objects and the information produced in the optic array that is sufficient for our knowledge of the world. Over the course of human evolution and of personal development, it is argued, we have acquired the capacity to respond directly to certain 'invariant' patterns of energy distribution in the input to the visual system. It is a view of perception that emphasises a direct response to well selected information. As we have indicated, Buddhist meditation induces a style of perception in which this kind of direct responding comes to predominate over constructivist perception. However, it has been suggested that theories of direct perception really square better with classical accounts of meditation in Hindu Yoga than with the Buddhist system.[15] It is intriguing to find some aspects of this modern debate between perceptual theories anticipated in the contrast between Hindu and Buddhist theories of meditation. Perhaps it is an unresolvable debate. Certainly it appears that accounts of meditative perception can be developed from either point of view.

It is probably an oversimplification to conclude, as Deikman does, that meditation induces a passive perceptual style. One line of research evidence that alerts us to this arises from investigations of the effects of meditation on perceptual style. Some of the measures used have been of how 'field-independent' or 'field-dependent' people are in their perceptual style.[16] In a typical task to measure this aspect of perceptual style, subjects are shown the outline of a vertical rod and a square frame in a darkened room so that only the rod and frame are visible. Either the rod or the frame may be tilted, and the subject's task is to judge which corresponds to a true vertical, a difficult task since the mind appears programmed to use the frame as a criterion and judge the rod in relation to it − that is, there is a tendency for judgements to be influenced or 'dependent' on the more salient aspect of the visual 'field'. Subjects who are more distracted by the frame are more 'field dependent' whereas subjects who are better able to ignore the frame in judging the tilt of the rod are called 'field independent'. Though such measures are probably influenced by extraneous factors such as intelligence, they provide a useful way of measuring something closely related to active and passive perceptual styles. The 'active' style is to be able to ignore the apparently vertical frame, the 'passive' style simply uses the visual information given, and tends thereby to be more 'field dependent'. The evidence is clear in showing that practising meditation makes people more field-independent (i.e. more active) in their perceptual styles.[17]

It is possible that it remains an oversimplification to polarise the debate into active vs. passive. There is probably much more variation in the style of perception that meditation induces. Some approaches require considerable imaginative effort. An interesting example is Goethe's method of 'exact sensorial fantasy' (though the connotations of fantasy are misleading here).[18] His principal application of the method was to meditate on plant forms. The first stage could be to form clear images of the series of leaves on a plant, and then to use imagination to think through the changes in forms until it became possible to actually see the process of metamorphosis of the leaf form. The perceptual style involved in an imaginative exercise such as this can hardly be described as passive. But, on the other hand, neither would an active, field-independent style be conducive to the perception of metamorphosis. The perceptual style involved does not fit easily into the dichotomy of active or passive.

We began this section by listing the various ways in which authors had attempted to describe the mode of perception involved in aesthetics and empathy. By examining work on how perception proceeds both normally and under conditions of meditation the distinction between *'analytic'* and *'nonanalytic'* styles can be more explicitly drawn. The analytic style is more active, and is less dependent on the 'field' – the immediate perceptual context which is normally used to judge various perceptual sub-elements. The non-analytic style is more passive and is more field-dependent, being less able to prevent attention being caught by the stimulus context and thus using it to make other perceptual judgements.

How do these distinctions relate to aesthetics and empathy? The research on aesthetics has not been done, but studies have examined how people of different perceptual styles differ in empathy. It has become clear that neither perceptual style by itself is sufficient. Two separate empirical studies have examined the relationship between empathy and field-dependent (i.e. passive) and field-independent (i.e. analytic) perceptual styles, and come to the same conclusion.[19] The results were the same in both cases. The majority of highly analytic people are cold, aloof and uninterested in people. Passive people, though they tend to be more sociable, are generally not truly empathic but simply conformist and approval seeking. In contrast, empathic people combine an analytical perceptual style with 'emotionally soft' qualities that are the opposite of those found in most analytic people. The hybrid style involved here, like Goethe's exact sensorial fantasy, does not fit easily into a simply dichotomy between passive and analytic. Indeed the imaginative effort needed to perceive the metamorphosis of leaf forms may not be dissimilar to that needed for empathy with other people. There is some experimental evidence that the daily practice of Zen meditation over a period of a month resulted in a greater improvement in accurate empathy than was found in a control group of non-meditators over the same period.[20] How does meditation have this effect? It appears that the basic style of perception experienced *during* meditation is a *passive* one, but that meditation makes people's *subsequent* perceptual styles more *analytic*. It is a paradox that meditation may involve the employment of a very passive style which allows an increasingly analytic style to be used subsequently. Such alternation between polarities can be a useful preliminary to the integration of aspects of the extremes into a single unified style of functioning. It is possible that this is what helps meditators to achieve the hybrid style that is conducive to empathy.

## Perceptual style and personal behaviour

Does learning to be empathic and to appreciate art affect behaviour outside the immediate aesthetic or interpersonal context? It will become clear how this may be the case if we examine how people acquire a sense of what they ought to do, how they develop a moral sense.

The most widely accepted psychological account of moral development is that of Kohlberg.[21] It is a theory organised around a series of developmental stages. According to Kohlberg, moral development proceeds through three general levels. At the first, 'pre-conventional' stage, there is some responsiveness to conventions of what is right or wrong, but it is based entirely on the physical power of the source of the rules and on the personal consequences of following them or breaking them. At the second, 'conventional' stage, the value of moral conventions is recognised, and the individual is not only guided by them but plays a part in maintaining them in the social community. This in turn gives way to the third, 'autonomous' stage in which self-chosen general ethical principles are interpreted in the light of particular circumstances.

This theory is inspired by Piaget's general views of cognitive development described in chapter 2, and emphasises the cognitive basis of morality. Some critics of this theory have argued that it gives too important a role to rational, analytic cognition, and neglects the role of the kind of non-analytic cognition which is found in aesthetics and empathy. Indeed, a number of parallels can be drawn between aesthetic and moral cognition,[22] i.e. they avoid stereotyping, they draw on a variety of perspectives and take up fresh vantage points, they demand genuineness on the part of the perceiver, and they involve the discernment of what is 'fitting'. Malcolm Ross has gone further[23] and suggested that both map closely onto the conceptualisation of love drawn in St Paul's first epistle to the Corinthians (chapter 13). One can thus argue that there are similarities involved in the kind of 'attention' that is involved in aesthetics, morals and in Christian love.

This analysis completes the circle, for it is very reminiscent of Simone Weil's concept of attention with which we started this chapter. After talking about academic study and the love of God, Simone Weil extended her concept of attention to love of the neighbour. It is a view of morality that has been taken up and developed by Iris Murdoch.[24] She complains that philosophical accounts of morality have tended to emphasise the role of the will in making moral decisions, both in Anglo-Saxon linguistic philosophy and in continental existential philosophy such as that of Sartre. It is an approach to morality that she rejects as being based on philosophically unconvincing arguments, as setting up a view of human nature that is empirically implausible, and as being morally objectionable. Her alternative account of morality, emphasising its perceptual features, explicitly borrows from Simone Weil the concept of 'attention'. She sees the central moral task as being 'to see justly, to overcome prejudice, to avoid temptation, to control and curb imagination, to direct reflection'. This requires 'attention', the same 'just and loving gaze directed upon an individual reality' as Simone Weil describes in the religious life. Once a person has learned, through 'attention' to see things as they are, it will be obvious what needs to be done. It is accurate perception, not correct resolution, that she regards as the central moral task.

## Religious and psychotherapeutic insight

With this background, we can develop the analogy that we introduced briefly in the last chapter between religious knowing and the way in which people acquire new insights about themselves in the course of personal psychotherapy. It is an analogy that will enable us to recapitulate some of the points that have been made already about the nature of religious cognition, but also to go beyond our previous analogues in one important respect.

Many of the insights that arise in psychotherapy concern the influence of key incidents (or groups of incidents) in our personal development, and the surprisingly pervasive influence these can have in shaping our attitudes, emotional responses, and ways of dealing with stress. Though such insights into personal development are potentially available to everyone, individuals may differ in the ease with which such insights are made explicit.

Secondly, their truth value does not seem to be as clear cut as, for example, a principle in physics or engineering. Personal insights are rational, but not in the same way as scientific hypotheses. They are not so tightly determined by evidence as scientific hypotheses, but neither are they independent of the relevant facts. In this they are also like our other analogues of religious cognition. A 'reading' of a work of art, for example, is to some extent personal. It is not wholly determined by the work of art, but neither is the viewer free to see whatever he chooses in it. His interpretation is circumscribed by the object he is viewing, to which he must be faithful.

Further, insight in psychotherapy seems to be necessarily accompanied by feeling. It is relevant here to note that there are different ways in which one can recall key autobiographical events. One can recall simply *that* something happened, or remember it actually occurring.[25] It is the difference between, for example, remembering going on a train as a young child and remembering merely *that* you went on the train. Personal insights do not generally seem to arise from merely remembering what has happened. They come, rather, from remembering the experiences sufficiently vividly that one can re-experience what one felt at the time. Such emotional recall seems to be necessary to understanding more deeply the significance of key autobiographical episodes. But, more generally, the process of acquiring fresh personal insights in psychotherapy seems to involve a degree of emotional involvement and personal commitment. Key events need to be pondered and reconsidered repeatedly before they yield their full significance. Personal insights only come from focussing on oneself in a sustained way with the kind of 'attention' that Simone Weil and Iris Murdoch have described in other contexts.

Personal insights gained in psychotherapy also carry implications for behaviour. If a client claims to have had a personal insight but finds it makes no difference at all to how he or she reacts in thoughts, feelings or behaviour in a previously upsetting context, the therapist would be inclined to doubt whether a genuine personal insight had been obtained. Of course there may need to be much determined effort before the insight changes old habits, but some 'shift' should be discernable. Similarly, it is a recurrent strand in all religious teaching that anyone who claims to know and love God, but who shows no evidence of this in his life, is a charlatan. Not that religious people are consistently 'good' or better than many others who are not explicitly religious. However, genuine religion clearly carries moral and behavioural obligations.

These two last aspects of psychotherapeutic insights, its involvement of emotion and its implications for personal change, have been intertwined together in an interesting distinction between two different forms of insight. Psychoanalysts have often made a distinction between two different kinds of insight that can be obtained by patients in therapy. It is a topic that was not much considered by Freud himself, but has been developed by a number of subsequent writers.[26] The contrast is between insight that is merely intellectual or neutral and a second type of insight that has been variously described as true, effective, dynamic or emotional.

Merely intellectual insight is of little therapeutic value. A therapist can put a novel idea to the patient about his problems, the idea can be correct, and the patient can accept it as such, but all this is not enough to give it any therapeutic value. Effective insight depends on more than this. To be effective an insight needs to be thoroughly assimulated and needs to be 'emotional' in the sense of being capable of arousing emotional reactions. Notice that the same idea could be either an intellectual or an effective insight. It is a distinction relating to the quality of the insight rather than its content. In a very different, religious context, Cardinal Newman made a somewhat similar distinction between whether propositions are held in a 'real' or a 'notional' way.[27]

The other important line of thinking in psychoanalytic theorising about the differences between intellectual or effective insight turns to the *grounds* of these insights. The proposition to be examined is that there is an experiential basis for effective insight that is characteristically not found for intellectual insight. Gendlin has provided the fullest and most general discussion of this claim.[28] He suggests that in intellectual insight, patients have a 'symbolisation' (i.e. an articulate conceptualisation) of their problems, though this symbolisation is not based on experience and so does not correspond to any 'felt meanings'. The reverse situation can also arise in psychotherapy. Patients sometimes refer to a powerful emotional experience without as yet being able to indentify the emotion or the cause of it ('... I feel very stirred up about something at the moment, but I am not sure what it is' ...). Gendlin would say that in this case there was a 'felt meaning' without any 'symbolisation'. In Gendlin's terminology the moment of effective insight occurs in psychotherapy when felt meanings are symbolised. Characteristically it is those experiences that are most difficult to symbolise that provide the most powerfully therapeutic insights.

There is nothing unique to psychotherapy about this sequence of unsymbolised experience leading to a moment of insight when symbolisation is eventually achieved. Creative discoveries are also characterised by a similar hunch or intimation that something new is about to be discovered when the matter has been thought through.[29] The pre-insight stage may be less emotional than in psychotherapy, but that simply reflects the different content of the insight and does not necessarily imply any difference in the process involved.

It is now possible to see a little more clearly how these psychological concepts map on to religious understanding. Contemplative religion has a long tradition of emphasising the role that is played by such unsymbolised, or at least very incompletely symbolised experience. Following the initial unsymbolised experience, there follows a struggle to cast it in a form in which it can be articulated and communicated. This is a difficult and demanding task, but not necessarily more so than the articulation of initially unsymbolised insights in psychotherapy. In this process of articulation, the contemplative of course draws on the thought forms current in his social and religious context.[30]

Though articulation of unsymbolised insights is possible it is often not without cost. Frequently, insight in its articulated form seems to do scant justice to the initial unsymbolised experience, thus making the effort at articulation an endlessly frustrating one. Articulation always involves conceptual distinctions, whereas the experience they are seeking to describe is, as Eckhart put it, 'a simple core which is the still desert onto which no distinctions can ever creep'.[31] It also seems that articulation robs the initial insight of some of its emotional power. In this sense, also, articulation is done at some personal cost. Nevertheless, the compulsion to articulate unsymbolised experiences, if only to assimilate them better oneself, seems to be strong. Hence, the voluminous mystical literature describing the unknowable.

We take the path of 'un-knowing' in Christian contemplation as reflecting these facts about the difficulty of articulating raw insight. In the Eastern Church, this path of un-knowing, the apophatic way,[32] has been given particular prominence, though Western Christianity has also had a similar 'negative' way. It was, after all, a mediaeval Englishman who wrote the mystic classic *The Cloud of Unknowing*.[33] Of course this path of 'not-knowing' is by no means confined to Christianity. Indeed it is probably more characteristic of Zen Buddhism than of any other religion. However, we have chosen to make our point in connection with Christianity because it is often not appreciated that the path of not-knowing has a place in Christianity at all. We can now see that the path of 'un-knowing' can be conceived as the achievement of a kind of religious experience in which one refrains from symbolising anything to more than a minimal degree.

The analogy between the unsymbolised experience of mystics and of patients in psychotherapy is strengthened by detailed features of the descriptions of wordless emotional experiences sometimes given in psychotherapy. A client described to one of us how, after the death of his sister, he went through a period of being greatly preoccupied with the loss and of thinking repetitively about it. However, after a while he reached a point where this kind of thinking ceased, and there was just an 'inner darkness' that was 'beyond words' and, paradoxically, was both 'light and dark at the same time'. The paradoxical sense, often described by the mystics, of coming to know something that is in a sense 'beyond knowledge', something simultaneously both light and dark does not appear to be specific to religion. We take the sense of 'unknowability' described by the mystics, not as showing that it is impossible to know God, but as describing a common aspect of the subjective experiences of religious and other related forms of personal knowing.

We wish to emphasise here the difference between, on the one hand, religious insight that has little experiential basis and, on the other, religious insight that arises from an effort to symbolise personal religious experience that was initially unsymbolised. Our suggestion is that in the former we have something that parallels merely intellectual insight in psychotherapy, whereas with the latter we have something parallel to effective insight. Religious insight that, like therapeutic insight, has been chiselled out of experience will have more personal consequences than merely intellectual or 'notional' religious insight. Emotional and behavioural reactions are more likely to be congruent with beliefs that have been formed in this way. Even a casual experience of contemplative religious literature would reveal the extent to which an insight into the nature of God and a passionate love of God are bound together. Also, the behavioural consequences of religious experience can be very marked and lead, either suddenly or gradually, to a transformation of lifestyle and personality. All this follows straightforwardly from the analogy with therapeutic insight.

With both personal and religious insight, the attempt to become conscious of 'felt meanings' and then to find ways of articulating them demands a special quality of attention that combines elements of both passive and analytical styles. Indeed, this is true of all the analogues of religious cognition, that we have discussed in this chapter. All involve a special combination of intellectual restraint and cognitive effort.

# 6

wwwwwwwwwwwwwwwwwwwwwwwwwwwwwwwwwwwwwwwwwwwwwwwwwwwwwwwwwwwwwwwwwwwwwwwwwwwwwwwww

# Emotional regulation and religious attentiveness

It will be clear from what was said in the last chapter that religious knowing involves an emotional component. As with aesthetics and empathy, religious cognition uses emotional responsiveness as an organ of knowledge, and does not depend solely on intellectual apprehension. We saw in the last chapter that aesthetic perception of a painting, involves both the restraint of impulses aroused by the work of art, but also a sympathetic emotional response.

In this chapter we consider the various roles which the emotions have played in the meditative, religious tradition. Psychological processes in meditation training will be reviewed, and the problem of emotional control raised. Finally we will draw some parallels between religious and clinical approaches to emotional control.

Many religious activities involve elements that seem intended to have an impact on the emotional state of the practitioner. The methods used to induce these states vary considerably.[1] Ceremonial, music, dance and oratory are commonly found. They can combine to produce a state of emotional excitement in which the quality of religious experience is heightened. Alternatively, religious experience may be associated, not with excitement, but with an unusual degree of tranquillity. This is true of most meditative approaches to religious experience, whether Western or Oriental.

Historically, religious experience through emotional excitement is probably older than the more meditative approach. The emergence of this approach can be traced in the books of the Old Testament.[2] In early Hebrew history there is an almost complete identification of religious inspiration with extraordinary and impulsive human actions. This is equally true whether it is compulsive, prophetic utterance or courageous battle deeds that are being considered. Early Israelite prophecy appears to have been associated with deliberately stimulated frenzy or ecstasy (1 Sam 10:5,6), and the book of Judges contains many identifications of religious inspiration with the excitement of battle.

One of the markers of the transition is the familiar story of Elijah on Mount Horeb (1 Kings 19:11–12) who recognised that the voice of Yahweh was not in the gale, the earthquake or the fire, but in a low murmuring sound. It was a view that was strikingly novel at that stage of Hebrew thought. Gradually, during the period described by the Old Testament the voice of Yahweh ceased to speak with its early regularity and force.[3] As the voice became more difficult to hear, it was increasingly necessary to become still and quiet in order to hear it. There thus developed an approach to religious experience through the cultivation of a state of tranquillity rather than through emotional excitement. Indeed a widespread development in man's approach to religious experience seems to have occurred around this time. It was in the sixth century that the Buddha was teaching in Northern India the approach to enlightenment through meditation.

However, there was no sudden break with the old experience of a strong prophetic voice. The independent Hebrew prophets such as Amos and Hosea, whose writings and sayings are recorded in the Old Testament, appeared to rely less than the 'official' institutional prophets of the cult and court on abnormally heightened emotion, ecstasy or visions to receive the word of God (Micah 3:5–8). They appear to have been more in the tradition of Moses with whom God spoke 'mouth to mouth, clearly, and not in dark speech' (Numbers 12:8). Both traditions (of excitement and tranquillity) have persisted alongside each other, and are often found intertwined. St Teresa of Avila in the sixteenth century shows in striking form a disciplined practice of silent meditation and the ecstatic emotion associated with her 'love affair' with the Christ. The two traditions continue side by side in the twentieth century where religious renewal is associated both with the emotional vigour of the charismatic movement and the disciplined attentiveness of meditation.

Since in this book it is with the contemplative aspects of religion that we are most concerned, we shall examine here the role of emotion in meditation. We start by examining psychological factors associated with the process of meditation itself.

### Psychological processes in meditational training

Two important features of all meditational trainings are a lowering of physiological arousal and the acquisition of a capacity for sustained attention. There is a clear relationship between these two, and the lowering of arousal can be seen as a necessary adjunct to attentional training. There are many similarities in the meditative paths recommended by different religions. Most recommend physical stillness, sustained concentration and emotional calmness. These are as much part of Buddhist training in concentration and mindfulness as of the 'via purgativa' in the Christian tradition.

However, there is considerable variety among meditational practices in the emphasis on physical factors, though the Western Christian tradition has given it less emphasis than Oriental traditions. Different schools advocate different positions for meditation. It has been argued that these positions create a balanced arrangement of the body, including a straight spine, which is helpful in producing muscular relaxation over a prolonged period. Whether or not there is any unique advantage in such traditional positions, (perhaps many of these who learn meditation are over-ready to take over such techniques without appraising their value, and inclined to give disproportionate emphasis to these physical aspects of meditation), it is nevertheless clear that meditation produces measurable physiological changes. Whether it is Yoga, Zen and Transcendental Meditation, or Christian contemplation, research has normally demonstrated a slowing and synchronisation of electrical rhythms in the brain, decreased and stabilised skin potential (a measure of very small changes in perspiration from the skin surface) and a slower breathing rate.[4] All these changes are consistent with a general state of lowered arousal and slower metabolism.

It is common ground among scientists that such physiological changes occur. What is doubtful is whether meditation has any *unique* physiological effects. Both those who are sympathetic to meditation[5] and those who are more cynical about its value[6] agree that other forms of relaxation produce similar physiological effects to those of meditation. There may of course still be unique non-physiological effects of meditation, cognitive effects for example, but any unique value that meditation may have does not seem to lie in the physiological domain. Nevertheless, the physiological aspects of meditation may provide a necessary background for its effects in other domains. In particular they may contribute to the changes in attentional processes that also result from meditation.

In normal states of consciousness, attention switches rapidly from one matter to another. This switching is exacerbated by stress. The sequence of imagery reported by people who have recently undergone stressful experiences is one of a rapidly changing, disjointed sequence of images.[7] A similar conclusion emerges from Jerome Singer's extensive studies of day-dreaming which have shown that there are three general dimensions of fantasy life.[8] Although the first of these is positive (the creative use of vivid fantasy life, associated with positive attitude towards it), the second and third dimensions are not. For the second common role for fantasy life is preoccupation associated with negative emotional states such as guilt, and the third is a state of distractibility, associated with anxiety and tension, in which fleeting, disjointed and poorly developed imagery predominate.

It is a common feature of all meditative methods that they seek to replace these negative and/or fleeting images by an ability to focus on single thoughts or sounds or activities. The aim is to focus attention on these alternatives tenaciously over a long period, and to learn to resist all other intrusions in the stream of consciousness.

Psychological studies have shown that there is a close relationship between the level of physiological arousal and the 'tenacity' of attention. The more aroused a person is, the more likely attention will switch rapidly from one thing to another. Sheer reduction in this arousal, such as takes place in meditation, helps the attention to remain for longer on any single element. Physiological relaxation helps sustained attention, but sustained attention also aids the arousal-lowering process.

A variety of techniques of practising sustaining attention have been employed in meditation. Perhaps the best known are the focus on breathing in Zen Meditation and the focus on a mantra in Transcendental Meditation. However, it is possible to compile a long list of others including external objects such as the cross, a vase or a mandala, parts of the body such as the abdomen or bodily processes such as breathing or the heart beating, or internal focuses such as visual images, phrases chanted aloud, a silently repeated mantra, humming, a prayer or a Zen Koan.

What is the significance of the focus that is chosen for meditation? Though each school of meditation puts forward arguments in favour of its own preferred focus, it is difficult to make an empirically based appraisal of such claims. In any case, it should be remembered that what is appropriate in one culture may not be appropriate in another.

In nearly every school of meditation it is regarded as important that the meditator should bring himself back to his chosen focus of attention when his mind wanders. The student of Zen Meditation, for example, who finds his thoughts wandering from the breathing process on which he is trying to focus, learns to bring his thoughts back again. There is some variation among techniques in the rigour with which intrusive thoughts are excluded, but frequently a rather gentle approach is advised. The meditator may be advised to simply 'neglect' the intrusive thoughts and return to the chosen focus.

It is significant that the emphasis is more on maintaining continuous attention on the chosen focus than on excluding competing thoughts. Intrusive thoughts may be permissible provided they do not disrupt the chosen focus. Indeed, it is one of the interesting features of the mode of attention that develops in meditation that it becomes possible to observe other thoughts with a 'detached equanimity' while maintaining attention on breathing or whatever is the chosen focus. Meditative attention can thus encompass other thoughts as well as the focal one. We have already referred to the fact that lowered arousal helps attention to be sustained. Research has also shown that relaxation can help to broaden the focus of attention. Under stress, attention becomes more narrowly focussed as people become more highly aroused.[9] The significance of these two effects of relaxation (increasing the capacity for sustained attention and increasing its 'bandwidth') for the style of perception associated with meditation will be developed in a later chapter on religious concepts, but it can be said briefly here that religious concepts are typically metaphorical, and involve seeing relationships between disparate things. 'Broad-band' attention seems likely to be conducive to this.

### Emotional control

Although meditation clearly involves the reduction of physiological arousal so that a person may be better able to sustain attention, all teachers of contemplative and meditative approaches have recognised that there are many hurdles to overcome in the practice of meditation. For example Augustine Baker, a seventeenth-century Benedictine, used his long experience as a spiritual director to make quite exact observations about methods of following the spiritual life, concentrating particularly on its early stages. His pragmatic and surprisingly modern approach to the regulation of emotional impulses is evident for example, in the way he introduces the spiritual life in *Holy Wisdom*:

There are two general impediments that nature lays in our way to hinder us from attending to God. The first is distracting images; the second, unquiet passions.[10]

In the twentieth century, Rudolf Steiner, among others, has taken a similar approach:

In a proper school of spiritual training certain qualities are set forth that require to be cultivated by one who desires to find the path to the higher worlds. First and foremost, the pupil must have control over his thoughts (in their course and sequence), over his will, and over his feelings.[11]

We will refer again in this chapter to Baker and Steiner as representatives of a 'modern', pragmatic approach to meditation. Traditionally various different ways of coping have been developed to deal with the distractibility associated with various aspects of emotional arousal. The aim of many techniques has been to subjugate the body so that the mind might be freed. The fourteenth-century mystic and ascetic Suso wrote about himself:

He was in his youth a temperament full of fire and life; and when this began to make itself felt it was very grievous to him; and he sought by many devices how he might bring his body into subjection.[12]

The devices were extreme. He describes, for example, a very tight undergarment that he wore at night, on which he fixed 150 sharp brass nails pointing towards the flesh. Meditation has often been thus associated with a moral dualism in which evil is associated with the material world or with physical impulses.

These practices have aroused a great deal of antipathy. Many have shared the strong views about such ascetic practices expressed by William Blake in a letter to his friend Linnell.

I ... am very sorry for all such who may be led to such ostentatious exertion against their eternal existence itself, because it is mental rebellion against the Holy Spirit, and fit only for a soldier of Satan to perform.[13]

What does modern psychology make of such practices? One response is the one that follows from Freudian psychodynamics. As far as their origin is concerned, it would see them as arising out of unresolved conflict and pathological guilt about basic human impulses. It would also see the consequences of such self denial as being pathological rather than therapeutic. The impulses repressed in this way would simply find expression in other disguised and possibly more pathological forms.

This is a severe charge. The question is whether it should be believed. Some of the claims of Freudian psychology are of rather doubtful scientific status.[14] There has not been the kind of careful empirical study of the psychological consequences of such self denial for us to know exactly what these are. There is, then, no necessity to accept as correct the criticisms Freudian psychology would make of religious practices of self denial. Despite this, there are good general scientific grounds for supposing that self denial is an inappropriate way of learning any procedure. The motivational basis of this kind of training programme conforms to a punishment paradigm in which certain responses are followed by punishment, with a considerable degree of gratuitous punishment thrown in for good measure.

Research on learning processes have made it clear that there are important differences between reward and punishment based learning paradigms.[15] In the first place, punishment is often simply less effective, especially when the response being punished is strongly motivated. Further, punishment can be counter-productive and lead to a strengthening of the response being punished, especially when the response is motivated by anxiety. Finally, punishment can sometimes lead to a generalised suppression of all motivated behaviour which is clearly undesirable. There is thus a clear distinction to be made between the punishment of undesirable tendencies and a training programme undertaken for positive objectives. The latter is not open to the same criticisms as the former. Psychological theory asserts that a training programme aimed at attaining positive objects would produce more effective learning than one based on punishment of undesirable reactions.

## Positive approaches

The repressive approach to emotional impulses represented by Suso is not the only one found in contemplatives. It is a fundamental insight of much contemplative religion that good and evil are intertwined with each other and defy any kind of easy separation. There are many who have followed a contemplative path in a much more pragmatic spirit than Suso. He started from the view that his natural temperament was offensive to him. Others have argued that this is not a necessary assumption of the contemplative life; that it can be undertaken, not because one's present state is offensive, but because there is a possible alternative human condition that is regarded as more desirable and worth working towards. This approach has been increasingly evident in recent centuries and is clearly shown, for example, in the writings of Augustine Baker and Rudolf Steiner. Psychologically this represents a very significant development. The spiritual life can be undertaken out of free choice rather than out of guilt-ridden, moral compulsion. If the contemplative path involves attempts at self regulation these can be undertaken, not because of their inherent virtue, but simply because they are preliminary accomplishments that are necessary if further progress is to be made in the spiritual life. Meditation can be approached in a pragmatic, more matter-of-fact, more positive spirit.

This conclusion emerges from a unique and very thorough empirical study by Mallory of a group of nuns and friars of the Discalced Carmelite Order following the contemplative path set out by St Teresa

and St John of the Cross.[16] A distinction was made in the questionnaires completed by the Carmelites between 'mild' (i.e. positive)
ascetical views that emphasised the purifying effect of God's love, and
'strict' (i.e. negative) ascetical views that emphasised that the contemplative must reject all desires except the desire for God. Data
analysis showed that advancement in mystical prayer was closely
associated with positive ascetical views but not at all with strict
negative views. The only correlation of strict views was with adoption
of the ideal of the cloistered life. Reflecting on these findings,
Mallory suggests that the part of the formulation of the contemplative life in St John of the Cross that emphasises strict asceticism is
unnecessary and has no basis in the actual practice of prayer. On
the other hand, according to Mallory, St John gives surprisingly
little emphasis to the positive emotional involvement that appears
to be fundamental to mystical advancement.

Adopting a more positive approach will significantly affect the
psychological consequences of the contemplative path for the person
engaging in it. In particular, it may reduce some of the problems that
have often been reported by contemplatives. Many have described
with painful vividness the periods of 'aridity' through which their
spiritual life passes, times in which they have little sense of the presence
of God and no enthusiasm for the religious life. The extent to which
this occurs may depend on the extent to which religious attentiveness
is maintained by 'approach' to spiritual realities, or 'avoidance' of
distractions. Too much emphasis on the latter would be expected to
produce the general suppression of motivation, of which 'aridity'
seems to be the phenomenological expression. It should be noted
straight away that these cautions apply only to the *expression* of
feelings, not to *experiencing* them.

## Emotional control and conflict

Do these criticisms of asceticism and harsh self denial of emotional
expression imply that emotions be freely expressed? Neither Baker
nor Steiner advocated this opposite extreme. Consider, for example,
Baker's remarks on the control of anger. He emphasises the importance of 'not breaking forth into words of impatience' or 'designs of
revenge suggested by passion'.[17] Steiner makes similar remarks about
the importance of controlling the outward expressions of feeling.[18]
This may look like a recipe for 'bottling up' or suppressing the feelings
involved in a way that would have unhealthy psychological consequences. The implicit assumption is often made here that emotion

accumulates rather like energy, and that it needs to be released. If it is 'bottled-up' it can lead to inner tensions, 'spark over' into other activities etc. From this point of view, any programme for the control of the expression of feeling looks rather objectionable.

Though the idea of emotion as a kind of energy that needs to be released is very common, it is not one that has received scientific support. There are a great many detailed problems with the model of emotion as energy,[19] difficulties that multiply as the model strives for greater precision. However, the most central objection to be made in the present context is to the assumption that emotion is a homeostatic drive that restores equilibrium in the way that hunger and thirst do. Deprivation from food leads to hunger, which leads to the consummatory activity of eating, which in turn restores the drive state to equilibrium. However, if drives are classified into homeostatic and non-homeostatic ones,[20] emotional states must normally be classified as non-homeostatic. Expressing feelings often increases rather than reduces them, and intensifies the desire to find further opportunities to express them in future. This is best understood in relation to a specific example such as anger.[21] Psychological research has shown that expressing anger does not normally reduce the intensity of the feeling. Objections to the cautions of Baker and Steiner about the expression of emotions thus have much weaker support than might be imagined. People do not always feel better when they express their feelings, or worse when they do not.

But if people do not express their feelings, what is to become of them? Though spiritual advisers often caution against the open expression of feelings, they do not necessarily wish to see a sense of *conflict* developing over the control of feelings. It may well be that conflict over the expression of feelings can have adverse psychological consequences, whereas mere non-expression does not. If, for example, one has been wronged, one may well be plagued with intrusive thoughts about the event in question or the person involved. Pragmatic contemplatives such as Baker and Steiner would advise that the expression of the emotion is unhelpful, but they would certainly not advocate a conflictual suppression of the impulses and thoughts themselves. For instance, Augustine Baker is critical of other authors who recommend unnecessary suppression of emotional impulses.

As for example in case of an injury received, they advise that we should call to mind all the circumstances that are apt to kindle indignation and resentment; and as soon as the passion is inflamed, then to suppress it by consideration of the example of our Lord, and His precept of charity to enemies, of the dangerous effects of revenge, and the blessed rewards of patience etc.[22]

The passage in which he gives advice on how to deal with 'hurtful or pernicious' thoughts that come into the mind during sleeplessness stands in marked contrast to a repressive approach and is particularly felicitous. It captures well his gentle, measured approach.

... in case they be simply vain thoughts that then wander unsettled in his mind, let him not willingly pursue them, but rather neglect them. Whereas, if they be sinful imaginations, let him as well as he can, divert quietly his mind from them, and now and then without much force lift up his mind unto God, or use some familiar prayers, or say the beads without much forced attention ...[23]

Buddhism also has a measured approach to the control of unwanted thoughts, in which a series of techniques are tried in sequence. The meditant only goes on to the next when previous techniques have been tried. Only the *last* of the techniques advocated is to force the thought out of the mind. Four other steps are tried before this, (a) to think of a different, incompatible thought, (b) to ponder the effects of the troublesome thought, (c) to try to ignore it and (d) to reflect on the removal of the source of the thought.[24]

It is now possible to see exactly what the contribution of a contemplative such as Baker has been. The important insight was to realise that a person can easily get distracted into dealing with the *content* of whatever the emotional intrusion was. For example one could feel secondary anxiety about having sensual impulses and imagine that in order to deal with these one needed to punish one's body violently. Or one could feel upset by having an angry thought about another person and believe one had to take special measures to punish oneself for it. Implicit in Baker's approach is that it is best to ignore the *content* of distractions, whether they are physical impulses, angry thoughts, guilty thoughts or whatever. The emphasis is on the interfering effects that they all have in common, rather than on their specific content.

It is interesting that careful assessment of obsessional patients who are bothered by intrusive negative thoughts has recently shown that disturbance of their mood is secondary to their intrusive thoughts. If a person experiences the intrusive thought that he may have harmed somebody, much of the consequent distress arises not from the unpleasantness of the thought itself, but from secondary thoughts *about* the original thought. For example, he may experience the secondary thought 'I must be a really aggressive person to think like this', and thus come to have a great deal of guilt about the original thought. Therapy is now beginning to focus, not simply on controlling the thoughts themselves, but on dealing with this secondary anxiety about the content of the thoughts. Guilt about the thought will tend, if not checked, to lead to a general deterioration in mood state which will make further distressing thoughts more likely. Suso's repressive method of dealing with such intrusive thoughts and impulses takes their content too seriously, thus reinforcing guilt and anxiety arising from them, rather than reducing it. Baker's approach is more pragmatic and positive. It starts from the assumption that all people have many dark thoughts and impulses that they would rather not have and focuses, not on their content, but on their tendency to interfere with contemplation.

### Emotional sensitivity

All the above discussion has been about the *expression* of feelings. A plausible case can be made out that acquiring control of emotional expression can help to produce a state of psychological calmness that in turn facilitates the spiritual path. It can be argued that provided this is done in a positive spirit and without unnecessary conflict, it need have no adverse psychological consequences. However, *sensitivity* to emotional experiences is quite another matter.

Any suggestion that a healthy spiritual life can be built on a blunting of emotional sensitivities needs to be rebutted strongly. In the history of Christian spirituality there have been repeated outcroppings of such tendencies. One example is the seventeenth-century heresy of quietism, which advocated a kind of 'mystic death' in which there were no actions or desires. It is a tendency that has probably been more prominent in Oriental spiritualities.

Restrained emotional expression need not at all lead to blunted emotional sensitivity. Indeed the opposite may be the case. Steiner has some interesting remarks to make here:

The pupil shall by all means rejoice over what is joyful and sorrow over what is sorrowful. It is the outward expression of joy and sorrow, of pleasure and pain, that he must learn to control. If he honestly tries to attain this, he will soon discover that he does not grow less, but actually more sensitive to everything in his environment that can cause emotions of joy or pain.[25]

An authentic religious life characteristically brings a heightening of both joy and sorrow.

An analogy may help in developing the point that heightened emotional sensitivity and restrained emotional expression can co-exist. It is part of the technique of a psychotherapist to use his emotional responses to a patient as an organ of knowledge about the patient.

How the patient conducts the relationship will produce emotional responses in the therapist. This is known technically as the 'counter-transference', and parallels the patient's response to the therapist which is known as the 'transference'.[26] The skilful therapist learns to read his own feelings very sensitively, and to use this to help him understand the patient. However, the *expression* of his feelings to the patient is a very different matter. This needs to be calculated in terms of its effect on the patient. There are times when it is helpful for the patient to know how he is making his therapist feel, but also many occasions when this is unhelpful. There is nothing incompatible about the heightened emotional sensitivity, but restrained emotional expression, that a psychotherapist cultivates.

Aesthetic cognition, as we saw in the last chapter, also requires a combination of emotional sensitivity and emotional restraint. Without sympathetic emotional sensitivity to a painting, there is little prospect of being able to really 'see' it. However, it may also be necessary to restrain some of the cruder, initial emotional responses to it, in order to create the space in which a full response can come to fruition.

## Religious and clinical approaches to emotional regulation

Recent years have seen an increasing use of meditation outside the context of the mystical and contemplative tradition in which it was originally developed. The person embarking on a spiritual path has his own reasons for seeking emotional composure and enhanced powers of concentration, but these are qualities that are clearly of value in many other contexts. It is not surprising, therefore, that the methods of meditation have been used in a secular context to achieve similar ends. They have been used in particular as a means of helping people with emotional or personality problems to bring increased stability into their lives. It has been claimed that meditation can be an effective way of tackling a great variety of problems. One review of the scientific literature on the therapeutic affects of meditation concluded by suggesting it is relevant to tension states, anxiety reactions, psychophysiological disorders, chronic fatigue states, sleep disorders, addiction to drugs, alcohol or tobacco, paranoid tendencies, obsessional tendencies, minor depressive states, poor tolerance of frustration, blocks to productivity, inadequate awareness of personal feelings, and excessive submissiveness or dependency on others.[27]

This is a far-reaching claim! Unfortunately the evidence is largely of an unsatisfactory quality.[28] Many evaluations of the therapeutic effects of meditation are methodologically suspect. For example, they may fail to ensure the prior comparability of the people who undertake meditation with the comparison group who do not. So, if the meditators appear to do better, it may be because they were the kind of people who would be likely to have a good outcome regardless of what kind of treatment they had used. There is also the problem that the effects of meditation may be explicable to a large extent by the 'faith' in the procedure of those who undertake it, i.e. meditation may work for those who believe in it simply because they do so, but it may have no value for those who do not believe in it. Because of these problems, it is necessary to be cautious about claims that are made for the therapeutic effectiveness of meditation.

Nevertheless, it is welcome that there should be cross-fertilisation between the traditional meditational methods of bringing about personal change and other similar exercises for the regulation of behaviour, thoughts or emotions that have been developed by clinicians to deal with the personal problems of their clients. There are striking similarities between the two, and some of the related clinical techniques will now be considered.

A necessary preliminary to most techniques aimed at the regulation of emotional reactions is to become more conscious of these reactions, though the methods for doing this are very diverse. Some, including most approaches derived from psychoanalysis, emphasise qualitative observations about the exact nature of the emotional reactions. Thus, if a patient is concerned about his emotional reactions to a particular person it is necessary for him to observe those reactions with as much clarity as possible. For example, when working on the 'transference' reactions to his therapist, the patient needs to observe his reactions carefully and to report them as they occur. Techniques in the behavioural tradition tend to adopt a different approach in which the patient and therapist first decide together on what are the troublesome reactions. In a depressed person, for example, there might be thoughts of self blame. Some therapies, Ellis' 'Rational-Emotive Therapy' for example[29] have developed a systematic (perhaps over-systematised) list of 'irrational' thoughts that they look for in each patient. The task of the patient is then to observe as precisely as possible how often and in what context these thoughts occur.

Such self observation serves a variety of purposes. It is of intrinsic value in educating a person about his emotional reactions. Careful observation can increase emotional sensitivity, and emotional sensitivity (we have already argued) is a tool of certain kinds of knowledge. Secondly, if the emotional reactions are troublesome, the act of observing them may make them less so. Though this occurs quite commonly, it is not well understood either when it does so, or why. Psychoanalysis would offer an explanation in terms of the value of bringing previously repressed emotions into consciousness, but other explanations can be considered. Careful observation may induce a more matter-of-fact view of the troublesome reactions, and help the person to distance himself from them. Also, the person may spontaneously and effortlessly begin to control his emotional reactions as he becomes aware of them.

In the religious world, it is in connection with the Buddhist technique of 'mindfulness' that the most explicit parallels to these clinical techniques are found, as for example in the following passage from Gunaratna.

Practising mindfulness of thoughts is the cultivation of the habit of looking objectively at thought ... When (for example) thoughts of anger arise, one must be fully aware of this and tell oneself, 'Now look, a thought of anger has entered my mind.' By this introspection a subtle effect is produced. The angry thought loses its compelling nature.[30]

Of course, it does not always happen that troublesome thoughts are controlled by careful observation. However, a variety of cognitive-behavioural techniques have been developed to assist in controlling them,[31] some of which parallel quite closely religious techniques for controlling unwanted thoughts.

The techniques vary in detail, but they start from the same assumption that disturbing emotional reactions are accompanied by interpretations of situations that are unbalanced and irrational. Indeed these unbalanced interpretations may largely cause the emotional reaction. Thus, when people are anxious they worry about things going wrong, and when they are depressed they take a generally negative view of themselves, the world and the future. A first step in therapy is to help the patient identify the ways in which the anxious or depressive thoughts distort reality. Patients are taught to 'catch the thought' whenever they feel upset, to see how their emotional reaction is often determined not by the objective circumstance but rather by how they have interpreted it. When a patient has become adept at recognising negative thoughts and images, the therapy focuses on modifying them and their effects using either distraction or undermining their impact by considering alternative interpretations of the situation that has caused the upset. (Note that this step of the procedure is very close to the primary method used in Buddhism for dealing with unwanted thoughts – the introduction of incompatible thoughts.)

Part of the value of such clinical techniques for controlling emotional reactions is that they create the mental space in which the person can think about how to cope with his problems, rather than just worry about them. The two kinds of thinking differ in a number of ways. For example, realistic consideration of problems is under voluntary control; people can start it and stop it at will. Anxious and depressive thinking seems to be out of the person's control. Realistic thinking can move forward from one step to another (e.g. formulating a problem, thinking of possible solutions, choosing the best way). Anxious and depressive thinking does not have this linear character. Instead, it is repetitive and stereotyped.

## Concluding remarks

If emotional responsiveness is to be used as an organ of knowledge, as it appears to be in aesthetics and in empathy, then it clearly needs to be a responsiveness which is clear and distinct, which enhances rather than obscures the object of perception, be it an object of art, or another person. The evidence presented in this chapter suggests that there is much commonality between the ways in which psychotherapy aims to bring about personal changes and those advocated by contemplative writers. In particular they both aim to reduce the level of emotional distress so that people may more clearly see exactly what it is that disturbs them. Indeed, the need for *clarity* of focus is an important unifying theme. Such clarity involves a finely tuned role for the emotions, in which they are neither too blunted nor too intrusive, and the person is neither too detached from his emotions nor too involved with them.

We have seen how the approach of the ascetic is not consistent with what we know from psychotherapy to facilitate this goal. This is firstly because it uses a punishment orientated rather than reward based approach. Secondly, because it concentrates on the content of the intrusive thought – taking the thoughts to be a serious comment on a person's 'true' nature – it tends to exacerbate guilt.

By contrast, modern psychotherapy and the more pragmatic part of the contemplative tradition have urged that intrusions be allowed to diminish more naturally (be they in Baker's terms, 'distracting images' or 'unquiet passions'). Both approaches are predicated on the assumption, not that such thoughts are 'wrong', but rather on the pragmatic consideration that they distract from the kind of attentiveness that is conducive to progress either in psychotherapy or in meditation.

The importance of the regulation of the emotions in psychotherapy is to leave space for the person to think realistically how to cope with their problems. When the balance of emotional reactions is beginning to 'come right' in psychotherapy a person begins to see things in a new light. Not only do they see things in themselves they did not previously know existed, they see other people differently. They find themselves reacting differently, not because they feel they *ought* to, but rather because they have obtained new perspective, new knowledge. They have to come to know themselves, other people, and the world differently.

In a similar way, the central purpose of religious techniques for emotional control has been to leave space for the development of knowledge of the 'divine'. In religious meditation as in psychotherapy, there are cognitive changes that result from obtaining the right balance of emotional distance and receptivity – the quality of attention to the object of perception is affected, and this changes how the object is 'known'. In the next chapter, we consider in more detail psychological approaches to the 'self', and explore connections between knowing the self and knowing God.

# 7

# Self knowledge and knowledge
# of God

In this chapter, we will consider the relationship between knowledge of God and knowledge of the self. At several points already we have suggested that personal insights of the kind characteristically arrived at in psychotherapy involve cognitive processes similar to those involved in religious insights. It is therefore central to our argument to examine self knowledge in some detail. People can approach knowledge of themselves in different ways, and not all are equally similar to how people approach knowledge of God. We want to draw out here the kind of approach to self knowledge which is most similar to how people approache God. Intertwined with this is the question of what kind of approach to self knowledge religious people aspire to. The kind of approach to self knowledge often advocated in the religious life is probably also the one that is most similar to how knowledge of God is approached.

Clearly there can be different views within the religious tradition about the basis of any similarity in how self knowledge and knowledge of God are approached. One view would keep a clear distinction between the self and God, but suggest that the religious person develops a characteristic cognitive style that is applied in both domains. This may come about, either because a growing awareness of God influences how religious people understand themselves, or because their self knowledge influences their knowledge of God. A more radical view would be that God and the self are approached in the same way because they are, at least in part, the same thing. There are theological and metaphysical questions here that lie outside our scope. We are not concerned with the *actual* relationship between God and the self. Our purpose is simply to describe the kind of self knowledge that is (a) characteristic of the religious person, and (b) most similar to his knowledge of God.[1]

Before going into the details of these issues there is an important background issue to consider, which is a serious threat to any balanced treatment of religious thinking about the self. This concerns the massive change that appears to have taken place in recent centuries in human understanding of the self.

## Changing perspectives on the self

Many centuries have passed since the world's classic religious documents were written and though there has been some development of religious views over time, the tie to the classical documents remains strong. To comment on the problem that this creates is commonplace. How is one to present the essential aspects of the classical religious positions in a way that is accessible to modern man? The attempt to do so involves disentangling the essential aspects of classical religious positions from those that merely represent the thought-forms of the time in which the classic documents were written. If we contrast the experience of self portrayed in classic religious documents with the modern, secular approach, two different contrasts are confounded. A religious approach to the self is contrasted with a secular one, but also an archaic one is contrasted with a contemporary one. The two contrasts are difficult to disentangle.

Our problems here are heightened by the fact that historical changes in human consciousness, and particularly self-awareness, have received only rather patchy scholarly attention. However, recently there has been increased interest in the evolution of consciousness.[2] Changes in thinking about the self have been so vast that it is hard to believe that they have been changes only in how man has *conceptualised* himself. It seems likely that there have been accompanying changes in self *experience*, i.e. that there have been historical changes in human consciousness. Sadly, however, there is no generally accepted and coherent account of the development of self experience and it is beyond our scope here to advance one. A few notes towards such an account are all that will be possible.

In the twentieth century, at least in the West, man has become fascinated with himself in a way that is quite new. No previous age could have embraced the diverse wares of the 'personal growth' industry in the way that contemporary Americans have (with Europeans following closely behind). Victorian worries about the dangers of introspection[3] have been replaced by boundless enthusiasm for self knowledge. Restrained social behaviour has been replaced by the view that emotional self expression is essential to mental hygiene (though, as we argued in the last chapter, this seems to have been derived historically from a misunderstanding of Freud's theory of repression). Integrity and authenticity have been put forward as central moral values, especially in existentialist literature and philosophy, though it is not clear that this is seen as a realistic objective even by its advocates. Even Sartre felt that the existential consciousness had become socially disengaged in its search for personal authenticity to the point at which everyday reality had become 'nauseous'.[4]

Contrast the concept of 'sincerity' as it was understood in the eighteenth century, with its modern meaning of authenticity to see how views have changed. It used to mean merely something that was pure or unadulterated, and applied to things rather than to people (e.g. a 'sincere' fat).[5] The concept of 'being true to yourself' is a new one. 'Duty' has shown a similar shift from being originally based on the discharge of the responsibilities associated by society with one's station in life, to a broader concept of the individual's own assessment of their obligations.[6] To get back into a mentality where sincerity and duty have their old meanings is to glimpse a vanished world from which personal assessments, perceptions and experiences seem largely to be absent. Psychologists have often neglected the extent to which personal experience depends on the currently prevailing social assumptions, though this has begun to arouse increasing interest recently.[7] Perhaps one of the most telling shifts in semantics since the eighteenth century has been the way 'subjective' has done a volte-face from its eighteenth-century meaning of 'relating to the subject in hand' to its present one of 'personal'.[8]

Looking back just two centuries makes the point that self experience has changed a great deal, but things were not static before that. The Renaissance seems to have been another period of enormous psychological change, though more a change in the possibility of a distinctively personal perception of the external world, rather than a development in *self* consciousness of a modern kind. Personal imagination was cultivated and valued in a new way through Renaissance 'studia humanitatis'.[9] Owen Barfield[10] has argued that it was a pivotal period for the slowly developing cognitive capacity that enables man to bring his own perspective to the perception of the world. We can still feel something of the cultural earthquake that took place in Europe 500 years ago, a stirring of the sense of inwardness that has since developed far and fast.

Going back much further and jumping over many subtle developments, we come to a 'primitive' cognitive style in which there was little separation between sensory experience, thought and action, and little of the self–other differentiation that we now take for granted.[11] Psychological development seems to have consisted in part of the dissolution of undifferentiated perceptual unities.

These skeletal notes will serve in part just as necessary background for any consideration of self-knowledge that wishes to avoid gross historical naïvety. But there is also a specifically theological point to be made about the psychological development towards a greater sense of inwardness and subjectivity to which we have pointed. St Paul seems to have been describing a shift in thinking in this general direction when he contrasts the moral and religious thinking of the Old and New Testament periods, the contrast between 'the letter that kills' and 'the spirit that gives life' (2 Corinthians 3.6). In characterising the new dispensation as one of the spirit, Paul seems to be describing a new kind of inner religious experience. We see evidence for this also in the concept of conscience ('syneidesis'), a Hellenistic concept imported by Paul, to which he gives a deeper religious significance. Even in Greek thought, it was a relatively new concept.[12]

However, Paul was not simply doing a piece of descriptive psychohistory, attempting an academic characterisation of changes in moral and religious consciousness that he had observed taking place. He was also the advocate of the new dispensation, and wished to claim a central role for the Christ in making this new dispensation possible. The kind of psychological development towards inwardness that we have described may thus be not merely a hazard that the cautious academic must keep in mind in criss-crossing between old religious views about the self and theories of the self in contemporary psychology. Rather, these developments in self-awareness may themselves be a continuation of the new era of 'the spirit within' that St Paul attributes to the Christ.[13]

Whether or not this suggestion is accepted, particular importance in this chapter attaches to the views of religious thinkers who are also sufficiently modern to share the distinctively modern concern with psychological 'inwardness'. A thinker who occupies a particularly interesting place in history in this connection is Kierkegaard, one of the fathers of existentialism and also a deeply religious thinker. He stands at an important point in the historical process of adapting religious insights to an age of increasing inwardness. His contribution to psychology is also quite detailed and substantial[14] and we will make several references to it in the following sections.

## The relationship between God and the self

There has long been a tension inherent in the Christian view of the relationship between God and man. One element emphasises the closeness of the relationship, the other emphasises distance. We shall argue that where an individual religious person instinctively stands on this issue has far-reaching psychological consequences.

Much Christian teaching about the closeness of the relationship centres around the 'imago dei' doctrine, man as the image of God.[15] There are two strands in this. One is universalist, that humanity was created in the image of God, that all men and women are the sons and daughters of God. The other is salvationist, that people become increasingly conformed to the image of God in so far as they follow the Christian way. (A third strand, which does not directly concern us here, is about Christ as the supreme image of God.) The universalist and salvationist strands were not clearly distinguished in St Paul but, by the second century, Irenaeus made an attempt to systematise them. 'Image' was the term used for the property of mankind generally, retained after the fall; 'likeness' was used for a further property, lost at the fall but recoverable in Christ. There have been varying views about which aspects of man constitute the image of God. Many have emphasised the rationality of man, but there is no consensus that it is only in this respect that man should be regarded as being in the image of God.

Alongside this formal doctrine of humanity made in the image of God there has been a corresponding view of the spiritual life. One view emphasises that there is an element in human nature that is a reflection of God. In seeking to know this aspect of his own nature a person also comes to know God. This is a view that has been prominent in the teachings of the Fathers, and the spiritual path followed by the contemplatives over the centuries has been based on the assumption that there is an inner path that leads to God. In the twentieth century this has been articulated most clearly by the existentialist theologians. Tillich's doctrine of God as the 'ground of our being' is a contemporary and explicit statement of this view.

In tension with this view of this relationship between the self and God has been the doctrine of man as a sinner. Biblically, it is captured in the words of Peter to Jesus, 'Depart from me; for I am a sinful man' (Luke 5:8). In terms of doctrine, this view has emphasised that salvation can only result from God approaching people, that people are unable to find the resources for salvation within themselves. At the level of experience, it is emphasised that the further people advance along the spiritual path, what they discover within themselves is not any kind of embryonic divinity, but sinfulness and unworthiness.

Tillich puts the distinction attractively:

One can distinguish two ways of approaching God: the way of overcoming estrangement and the way of meeting a stranger. In the first way man discovers *himself* when he discovers God; he discovers something that is identical with himself although it transcends him infinitely, something from which he is estranged, but from which he never has been and never can be separated. In the second way man meets a *stranger* when he meets God. The meeting is accidental. Essentially they do not belong to each other.[16]

Though most religious people probably find they have a natural leaning to one side or the other of this polarity, our assumption is that the tension cannot be satisfactorily resolved in favour of one side or the other, but that both views need to be retained in a creative polarity. We shall argue that, at least from a psychological standpoint, this is the stance that has the most satisfactory consequences.

It may be helpful to offer a psychological analogy for the polarity between the relationship between the man and God. It comes from Jung's treatment of the polarity between the ego and the Self.[17] (We use 'Self' with a capital letter for Jung's concept, and should draw attention to the fact that in this analogy it corresponds to God.) For Jung, the ego is the centre of conscious experience. The 'Self', in contrast, is the centre of the whole personality, not just of consciousness. It exists on a higher moral level than the ego, and is the source of wholeness and integration. Its relationship to the ego is that of the 'mover' to the 'moved'. It is the purpose of the Self to bring the person to integration and wholeness. In this sense, Jung suggests, Christ serves as a symbol of the Self.

Jung is concerned that the 'axis' between the ego and the Self should function in a healthy way, and this involves maintaining a polarity between them. This can go wrong in one of two ways. The ego can 'inflate', become grandiose, and in a shallow and inadequate way, usurp and imitate the deeper functions of the Self.[18] Alternatively, the ego can be alienated from the Self, or crushed by it, so that it cannot develop properly in relation to the Self (as a child/adolescent may not develop properly if alienated from his parents). The analogy with the relationship between man and God will be clear. Man can become 'inflated' and usurp the functions of God, or he can become 'alienated' and disconnected from God. In both cases the axis between them malfunctions.

There is one last point to draw from this analogy. Jung's equation of the Self with the Christ puts him clearly on the side of those who have maintained that God can be found through an interior path. However, this does not commit him to grandiosity. Within his own framework, he found the need to re-invent the man–God polarity as an ego—Self axis. It is as misguided, in his framework, for the ego to usurp the place of the Self as it is in theology for man to usurp the place of God. Self knowledge *can* be 'grandiose' and 'inflated', but it *need not* be so. In Jung's framework the key question is not *whether* or not man looks within himself for the symbol of God, but *how* he looks.

## *Self-preoccupation*

Many writers have emphasised the lack of 'self concern' that characterises a religious approach to self knowledge. One of Kierkegaard's recurrent themes is the importance in the religious life of giving up self concern. A religious person has distinctive motives for self knowledge and distinctive attitudes to acquiring it. Kierkegaard is very clear that self concern is not a necessary accompaniment of knowledge of the self. Indeed he sees self concern as almost incompatible with knowledge of what he calls the 'true self', which has about it a directness and immediacy that he sees as standing in contrast to self concern. Some such view has been common in much Christian teaching about self-knowledge. The contemporary Jungian psychologist, James Hillman has made similar points in amplifying what he takes to be the distinction made by Bernard of Clairvaux between proper self knowledge which is the first step to humility and 'curiosity' which is the first step to pride (though it is possible that he is putting a modern gloss on the points made by St Bernard in the twelfth century).

St Bernard speaks mainly of its destructiveness in regard to oneself, of the harm the curious mind can have upon peace of soul and spiritual enlightenment. The ego, with its light, attempts to ferret out causes in hidden recesses of the personality, searches for detailed childhood memories, promotes sweet sessions of silent introspection. We are curious to know who we are and how we got this way, whereas the religious attitude would recognise from the first that we are God's creatures and we are what we are owing to His purpose working in the soul rather than to accidents of upbringing and circumstance. Interpreted in terms of depth psychology, St Bernard's caution means allowing the unconscious to come in its own way at its own time without trying to piece together in a curious fashion a case history as an explanation in answer to the question 'why?'[19]

Thus, Hillman sees the mistake of curiosity as lying partly in trying to force the pace of self-knowledge. Though there is value in establishing a desire for self-knowledge, it is a mistake to try to piece together all the answers too quickly. This will be reminiscent of points made in chapter 5. Goethe's observational method of 'exact sensorial fantasy' involves a similar suspension of premature discursive thought, as does the viewing of a painting. It was also remarked that the meditative mode of perception involves suspension of active perceptual processes which 'construct' a representation of what is in the sensory field. The 'apophatic' theology of the Eastern Church similarly involves learning to negate propositional statements about God, because they get in the way of direct spiritual experience. Inadequate conceptualisations distort actual experience of God. Here, in Hillman's interpretation of St Bernard's condemnation of curiosity, we find a related point about self knowledge. He is suggesting that if we are to come to know ourselves deeply and truly, we need to avoid trying to piece the story together hastily and prematurely. On this view, reverence would be characteristic of a proper approach to self knowledge as well as of knowledge of God. Knowledge of ourselves, as of God, must in a sense wait until things are disclosed to us. The pace and scope of both proper self-knowledge and knowledge of God are not wholly under our own control.

The motives that guide self-knowledge will also influence what we select from the range of personal phenomena that are available for attention. Some facts about ourselves may be interesting, but trivial in the sense that they tell us nothing 'important'. A reverential approach to self-knowledge eschews what is merely of curiosity value.

## Vocational approaches to self-knowledge

A recurrent theme in religious thinking about self knowledge focuses on the way in which the religious person discovers his identity by discovering his vocation. It will be useful to approach this idea by contrasting it with the two main approaches to personality that have dominated twentieth-century psychology. These two traditions in psychological theories of personality have developed rather separately, and only relatively recently have they really begun to make contact with each other.[20] One has been concerned with personality processes and development, the other with psychological traits and the regularities in individual differences in behaviour that they summarise. It is an issue on which, we will argue, there is a distinctively religious position.

In one tradition, there has been a lot of interest in the development of the self concept in childhood, and in the processes by which adults change or maintain their views of themselves. Freudian psychology has contributed theories of 'defence' mechanisms, for example how people show denial of extremely distressing or uncomfortable facts. Attribution theory has pointed out that the impact of successes and failures is moderated by how people interpret them, for example a failure in an examination that you put down to lack of effort has different consequences for your self concept than if you see it as resulting from lack of ability. (We will return to attribution theory at greater length in the following chapter.) These are examples of 'process' approaches to self knowledge.

In distinction, another branch of psychology has been concerned with taking a sample of people at a single point in time and seeking ways of classifying them. The classification of people into introverts or extraverts has been one of the most successful. There is clearly a kind of self knowledge that can be based on observing the relevant aspects of one's behaviour (sociability, impulsiveness, etc.) and comparing oneself with other people on these dimensions. The limitation of this approach to personality is that people's behaviour is not in fact invariable across situations. If someone is sociable in one context and quiet in another, how should they be classified? Nevertheless, trait concepts such as introversion−extraversion have been very useful in psychology and provide at least a partial explanation of differences between individuals on an impressive array of psychological variables.

However, neither of these psychological traditions adequately captures the approach to self knowledge to which the religious person aspires. In *The Sickness Unto Death*,[21] Kierkegaard develops an antithesis between the true and false self. The true self lives in agreement with the 'power which posited it' (i.e. God); the false self in contrast is one that the person 'himself has thought up'. The argument is that each person has a destiny for his life, though not one that can be laid out in advance. We have here a version of the doctrine of man as created in the image of God. The image is man's destiny. The particular way in which Kierkegaard develops this theme emphasises the 'self in becoming'. This approach probably comes partly from his general suspicion of 'knowledge', (on which his views were similar to those of Pascal mentioned in chapter 4) and partly from his emphasis on God as being beyond knowledge. For Kierkegaard, man's destiny is not something that he can discover in advance. God is like 'a deceptive author who does not write the outcome in large type or give it in advance in a foreword'.[22] Thus, there is a sense in which at any moment in time the self does not yet exist. Rather it is 'that which is to come into being'.[23]

We see here an interesting way of bringing into a single exposition a concern with the self as evolving process and the self as static identity. Self-identity is seen as something that can be discovered by varying degrees of approximation to an initially unknown template. The closer a person approximates to becoming the person represented in the template, the more he will find a sense of fulfilment. This is a general view about self-knowledge; there is nothing distinctively theological about it until one adds the proposition that God is the source of the to-be-discovered identity. The kind of approach to self-identity exemplified in Kierkegaard's position can thus be examined on its own merits from a psychological point, and has attractive theoretical features. Though not necessarily religious, it is readily compatible with a religious approach to self-identity.

There are some recent developments in psychological approaches to personality which are more readily compatible with the kind of approach implicit in Kierkegaard's thinking than are traditional psychological theories. An influential book, *The Explanation of Social Behaviour*[24] has served as a manifesto for a fresh approach to personality and social psychology, has adduced a range of arguments for approaching personality in terms of 'dispositions' rather than displayed characteristics. Dispositions differ from traits in that they are habitual styles of reacting to events, rather than invariable sets of behaviours. Vocation is a dispositional concept that is thus consistent with this new approach to personality.

The notion of discovering one's true self in conformity to an ideal pattern has found expression in the concept of vocation. It is a common observation that people who 'find their vocation' feel fulfilled. In finding it, they have discovered something important about their identity. Though some degree of sense of vocation is by no means uncommon, strongly 'vocational personalities' (as Emmet[25] calls them in a helpful chapter on the subject) are relatively rare. An interesting case is that of Florence Nightingale.

The story begins at seventeen when a religious call came in the form of 'voices'. The idea became implanted that she must give herself to some kind of work, though it was eight years before she became clear that this would be nursing. This was the thread that held the rest of her life together, a further period of eight years' preparation for nursing, her time of active nursing, and her final period advising on public health and establishing the professional training of nurses. It is clear in such a case how her vocation was the basis of her sense of self-identity, though she was not without other forms of self-awareness. The line 'I must try to remember that God isn't my private secretary' reveals an awareness of her tendency to coerce others into fitting in with her own plans and needs. We do not want to suggest that such *single-minded* vocations are common, that they are necessary for self-identity, nor even that they are desirable. In most people there is not so much a single, overriding vocation, as a network of intermingling vocational activities. Neither are vocational activities always undertaken as a result of a fully conscious decision; quite commonly people react instinctively in a situation that presents them with opportunities for vocational activities. It is only in retrospect that they may be identified as such. It may indeed be one of the key properties of vocational activities that they tend to be undertaken instinctively by a person whose life is appropriately oriented.

An assumption of the religious position would be that it is important to self realisation that opportunities for vocational actions should be grasped when they present themselves. Vocational activities may have the status of what psychologists have sometimes called 'developmental tasks'. In childhood, there is clearly a series of activities undertaken at different stages of development which serves to extend the individual's functional capacities. There seems to be an analogous sense in which in adulthood vocational opportunities are important for developing a sense of self-identity. The person discovers his identity only by grasping the opportunities that present themselves. They are the 'developmental tasks' of adult life, and may extend personal capacities as well as self knowledge.

The experience that identity is sometimes discovered only by undertaking development tasks is reminiscent of Kierkegaard's view that the true self is not discerned in advance but discovered in 'becoming', though Kierkegaard was probably over dogmatic about this, and the discovery of the true self probably proceeds along more varied routes than he recognised. Florence Nightingale seemed to be aware of her vocation before she took it up. Nevertheless, it is a useful observation that in some cases vocation is discovered *in the course of taking it up*. Perceiving the significance of life events and personal opportunities is an interesting and subtle matter that has an important place in religious prayer-life which we will consider more explicitly in the next chapter.

A final problem about vocational insights is their validity. When someone believes that he has discerned his vocation, can we speak at all of the insight being 'correct' or 'incorrect'? What are the criteria by which we are to judge the validity of vocational insights? These difficult questions parallel the equally perplexing questions that can be raised about the validity of personal insights generally, and about the validity of the 'interpretations' offered by psychotherapists,[26] and it may be helpful to approach the question of the validity of vocational insights from the perspective of this analogy.

It is clear that there is often inadequate evidence available by which to judge the validity of insights and interpretations in psychotherapy. However, this is no reason for concluding that validation is impossible. People occasionally, especially under stress, reach purported insights about themselves which are so wayward that we can confidently say they are incorrect. At the extreme, people can have ideas about themselves which are clearly delusional. This is sufficient to reject the notion that personal insights are in principle unverifiable, and that the concepts of truth and falsehood do not apply to them. However, there is probably no single criterion that is sufficient to justify the acceptance of such insights and interpretations. Certainly, the simple fact that they are affirmed by the person concerned, or that they make him 'feel good' is insufficient. Nevertheless, there are a variety of criteria, which, taken together, are better than nothing: the extent to which the insight is compatible with a wide range of facts about the person, the extent to which it is accepted over a period of time and under changing circumstances, and the extent to which it is fruitful in promoting personal growth. By using such criteria it is in principle possible to try to distinguish authentic from bogus vocational insights.

### Social and personal sources of self-knowledge

William James[27] divided the self that we know into the material, the social and the spiritual. He saw the social self as comprising such things as the recognition of people one loves, and the approval of peers, whereas the 'spiritual' self comprised psychological faculties and dispositions, will, and the stream of thought. Theories of self knowledge have had difficulty in taking a balanced view of the relative importance of social and spiritual (or introspective) components. There has been a tendency, though one that perhaps ought to have been resisted more strenuously than it has been, to build a theory of self knowledge entirely on one or the other.

Usually the emphasis has been on the social basis of self knowledge, and there have been two main contributants to this. One has been psychology's methodological coyness about dealing with introspection. This has led some psychologists to argue that people know themselves exclusively by observing their own social behaviour.[28] Academic psychology has generally put little emphasis on introspective sources of self knowledge. Similarly, sociologists, working in the tradition of the 'social interactionism' associated particularly with G. H. Mead, have emphasised that self knowledge is derived from the social context, especially from the opinions of others.[29] It has been disappointingly rare in psychology to find acknowledgements of *variability* (whether between people or between contexts) in the relative importance of social and introspective sources of self knowledge, and a willingness to study it empirically.

It might seem at first that religious approaches to self knowledge emphasise its private, introspective basis. Religious techniques of meditation are capable of producing marked increases in introspective awareness and there is a strong tradition in Oriental esoteric psychologies that withdrawal from ordinary experience through meditation leads to introspective knowledge of the 'true' or 'pure' self.[30] Among Western mystics St Teresa's account of her spiritual journey in *The Interior Castle* is clearly an account of deepening psychological awareness.[31] However, she makes little explicit claim that her spiritual journey involves increased self knowledge. Much less does she advocate undertaking the journey for that reason.

Though religion has often valued introspective self knowledge, Christianity at least has no wish to emphasise this to the exclusion of more socially based self knowledge. Indeed it will be fruitful to take the role of human relationships in self development as a model for the role of God in the self development of the religious person.

It is a psychological truism that self awareness and self realisation are achieved in the context of personal relationships. This is, in a special sense, also true of the religious person; though in this case it is the relationship with God which provides the essential context. In formulating the role such relationships play in the self development of the religious person it will be useful to recall the general, secular importance of the social context for personal development. The view that people have of themselves is arrived at in the context of social relationships. Most of the insights an individual has into the nature of his personality are essentially *comparative*. They are statements about the extent to which a particular trait or impulse is present. Such statements implicitly use a judgment about the extent to which the trait is present in the average person as a reference point (though such judgments are probably often distorted). A person arrives at a view of himself by comparing himself with various reference groups with whom he comes into contact, concluding that he is either like or unlike a particular type of person.[32]

Similarly a person's evaluation of himself is very largely based on how he values himself in comparison with other people, whether he sees himself as better or worse than others. There is an element of this in the way religious people think about themselves. However, the attributes of God become a more significant reference point against which the religious person appraises his own qualities. This can result both in a recognition that he is made in the divine image, and also in a sense of unworthiness in comparison with God. There is a danger, of course, that people with an overwhelming sense of arrogance or inadequacy will simply translate this into a similarly unbalanced view of their standing in relation to God. (This will reflect what, in Jungian terms would be seen as a malfunctioning of the ego–Self axis.) In other people, a balanced view of their relationship to God can help to liberate them from distorted comparisons of themselves with other people.

However, evaluation is a limited aspect of self knowledge, and the main contribution of a religious perspective to self perception does not lie at this level. Among the social relationships that are most important in developing a sense of self are those 'role relationships' in which people have particular contributions to make to a shared endeavour, such as occurs in marital relationships, work relationships, and parent–child relationships. Sociologists have often argued that people's self concept is largely based on the social roles people have, and that role relationships are crucial to the sense of self. The religious person also has something analogous to a role relationship with God. There is a common task (of the redemption of the world and of himself) on which the religious person is engaged with God, and his sense of himself will be based in part on his experience of this role relationship.

Whatever the context, there are two dimensions of role partners that are important, though the terminology varies.[33] Parents need to show both discipline and nurturance with children. Work supervisors need both to structure tasks and to show consideration. Psychotherapists need both to show support and understanding, but also to challenge and press for change. It seems to be important if people are to function effectively in role relationships, and to develop within them, that both of these should be provided. Personal development involves finding a balance between making demands on other people, and recognising their demands on oneself. Where this balance is not maintained, both social relationships and self development become distorted. Maintaining this balance in our relationships, Danziger[34] has argued, is achieved by internalising the balance between demands or supports shown by parents. Similarly, successful *re*socialisation through psychological therapy depends on the therapist providing the client with a balance between demands and support that can enable him to learn to maintain a better internal balance in future between his demands on other people and their demands on him.

The vocational role relationship with God seems to conform to this general pattern of providing a balance between demands and supports of a kind that facilitates personal growth and effective personal relationships. God is experienced by the religious person as someone who understands him perfectly and supports him constantly, but also as someone who makes considerable demands on him. The character-istic experience of the religious person is that, in the context of the experience of God's support and understanding, it becomes possible to rise to challenges and demands that might have been thought impossible. Just as rich human relationships are good for personal growth, so is the relationship with God felt to be so. The sense of expanded capacities that comes from operating in the context of a supporting/demanding relationship (whether human or divine) is also conducive to a balanced development of the sense of self.

## Self knowledge and personal freedom

One of the concerns aroused by a concept of a 'true self' such as that held by Kierkegaard is its implications for personal freedom and autonomy. On this point it may be interesting to compare it with Jung's concept of the Self, to which we have already referred. Whereas for Kierkegaard the true self comes into being in the process of being realised and adopted, for Jung the Self is something that has always existed.[35] However, Kierkegaard's position is really somewhat ambiguous. On the one hand, as he says in *The Sickness Unto Death*, the self 'does not actually exist; it is only that which is to come into being'.[36] Yet, on the other hand, the self is posited by God, and to become oneself is to do the will of God. In the *Edifying Discourses*, he holds up the bird and the lily as examples because they uncondition-ally do God's will, and adds 'You, too, are subject to necessity, of course; God's will is done anyway, of course, so strive to make a virtue of necessity.'[37] Which of these two possible positions about the pre-existence of the true self people prefer will depend partly on their general philosophical stance. But there may also be significant psychological consequences of which view is adopted. A 'true self' which is created as it comes into being may be felt as less of a threat to personal freedom.

There has long been some such tension in Christian thinking about personal freedom. On one hand, the Christian path is said to lie in conformity to one's *true* self (which can be equated with the will of God). On the other it is said to involve an experience of personal freedom. Augustine put it concisely when he said that the 'service of God is perfect freedom'. There have long been two such strands of thinking about personal freedom.[38] On the one hand, freedom can be contrasted with a state of affairs in which external constaints limit freedom of action. Alternatively, in rationalist philosophy as well as in religious thinking, freedom can be contrasted with internal constraints. The liberation that the religious life promises is from habitual patterns of thought or emotion to which people are said to be enslaved. Set free from these constraints, it is argued, people will be free to realise their true potential, to become the people they really are.

Clearly there are dangers in this latter notion of freedom. It can all too easily lead to coercive practices being carried out in the name of giving people their 'true freedom'. It can lead to arrogant claims being made about what people would wish to do if they were truly liberated, claims that bear no relation to the conscious wishes of those concerned. But these dangers arise when people slide illegitimately from talking specifically about freedom from internal, psychological constraints to talking about freedom generally. The former concept is a perfectly coherent one, provided it is not confused with other, broader notions that do not belong to it.

Indeed, the development of psychological awareness in the twentieth century has provided us with a much fuller concept of 'freedom from internal constraints' than we have had previously. The concept has acquired a vastly extended currency, and become the objective of almost every personal growth movement. Concepts such as enhanced self-awareness, self-realisation, development of personal potential are no longer esoteric concepts. It is a commonplace of the late twentieth century that personal freedom can be sought through release from personal 'hang-ups'. Yet this secular notion differs from the corresponding religious one in that it doesn't embrace the concepts of vocation and doing the will of God as the source of personal freedom.

The interesting psychological question that arises here is how an attempt to conform to the will of God avoids producing a sense that personal freedom is being inhibited. In psychological theory, the sense that freedom of thought is being threatened is said to produce a state of 'psychological reactance'.[39] This arises when one person finds his opinions, on a topic on which he feels he has some competence, disagreed with by another person. Psychological reactance is most likely to arise if the other person is in a position of authority, is not regarded as attractive, and tries, in a heavy-handed way and without discussion, to bring about a substantial shift in the first person's opinion. The result is usually that the person holds his original view even more strongly, or moves to a view even further removed from the other person's view than his original one. Consistent with this, people are less likely to implement decisions conscientiously if they have not been involved in making them. If they feel decisions have been forced on them they may assert their autonomy by subverting those decisions.

Now, it is clear that the sort of relationship a religious person has with his God is very different from relationships with coercive human authorities. The religious person's experience is of God within him, benevolently guiding him, in a continuing developing relationship. The religious position is neither of abject obedience nor of rebellion, but of living and working together with God, in a state of mutual indwelling. It would be no more likely to produce a sense of freedom being restricted by an outside agency than would be a close human relationship between two lovers.

Some twentieth-century psychologists, such as George Kelly, have seen freedom as residing in man's ability to think freely and originally about the experiences that confront him. 'Man, to the extent, that he is able to construe his circumstances, can find for himself freedom from their domination ... Theories are the thinking of men who seek freedom'.[40] Rudolph Steiner has taken up a similar position in his *Philosophy of Freedom*,[41] arguing that independent thinking is the basis of human freedom, a freedom that people do not have automatically, but one which they can acquire. Steiner believed that this capacity for independent thinking is the necessary basis for any valid spiritual development. In order to develop spiritual awareness, it is necessary to have the capacity to free oneself from conventional lines of thought. Steiner frequently contrasted this independent thinking with the vague mysticism that is often taken to be 'spiritual'. From his point of view there was no opposition between spiritual development and contemporary man's move towards social freedom and scientific discovery. All these have their basis in independent thinking.

The concept of conscience in Pauline thinking that we referred to earlier, illustrates the central place of personal thought in Christianity. It is very important, experientially, that the religious person who seeks to conform to God's will *for him* is not engaged in conformity to mere universal injunctions. Rather, he is involved in first constructing a view of the nature of his true self, and then living it. The fact of being involved in discovering the true self will affect how he perceives it, and his willingness to be guided by it.

Again, the Jungian concept of a person seeking insight into his true Self in psychotherapy will serve as a useful analogue. The goals of the Self are specific to the individual concerned, not general directives. The Self may be discovered in collaboration with a therapist. For example, dreams may be scanned for intimations of the goals of the Self, with the patient and analyst seeking together to interpret them through a cautious, collaborative process, not through the mechanical application of a deciphering code. Eventually a degree of insight into the nature of the Self is achieved through a laborious and creative process in which the patient is fully involved. By elaborating a new conceptualisation of himself, he can feel that he is winning his own freedom.

In this chapter we first considered the relationship between God and the self, and argued that this need not be taken either as one of identity or of total division. Jung's concept of the ego–Self axis was offered as one model for this relationship of the self to God. This kind of self knowledge is approached with seriousness of purpose, not on the basis of mere curiosity. We also suggested that the religious person tends to use a model of identity based on the process of 'becoming', and the concept of vocation was seen as illustrating in traditional language an approach to self-identity in terms of such an adoption of a true self. Next, we emphasised the role of socially based self knowledge, and suggested that the role of another human person in the development of self knowledge is an analogue of the role of God. Finally, we considered the relationship between self knowledge and personal freedom, emphasising that the 'cooperative' nature of the relationship with God from which a religious person's sense of self arises does not lead to an experience of the loss of personal freedom.

# 8

The interpretation of experience
in prayer

Close to the heart of religion is the development of a distinctive view
of personal experience. There is, of course, nothing exclusively
religious about the search for meaning in life; the quest to find
meaning appears to be a fundamental human instinct. Nevertheless,
these are distinctive features of the religious search for meaning.

Prayer is, amongst other things, the medium through which the
religious person engages in the interpretation of experience. The good
and bad things that have happened to us, the things we are inclined
to feel proud or guilty about, and our concerns and wishes for the
future, are all reviewed during prayer. Because of the particular
context in which they are reviewed, namely, the felt presence of God,
the review takes a particular religious form. Prayer thus provides
people with an opportunity to develop an understanding of the
relationship between God and their personality and experience. In this
sense prayer is a cognitive activity and it is this cognitive function of
prayer that will be considered in this chapter.

### The development of prayer

Our emphasis on this interpretative function of prayer will inevitably
lead us to focus on prayer of an apparently adult kind. However, as a
corrective to this, it will be helpful to begin by considering how prayer
develops and how, under stress, it may revert to relatively primitive
forms.

Goldman's research on the development of religious thinking in
children, described in chapter 2, yielded some rich and interesting data
about the development of prayer.[1] Rather than asking the children
about their own prayers he elicited comments from children by
showing them a picture of a child of their own age and sex praying
at a bedside. In this way the following aspects of prayer were investigated: prayer content (e.g. what do you think they are praying
about?); the purpose of prayer; failure in prayer (e.g. does their

prayer come true? How will the child know?); and God's presence in prayer. Overall, the results showed a development from 'crude, materialistic, egocentric' concepts to more 'defined, spiritual, and altruistic' concepts.

Three main stages were delineated. The first, lasting from 7 to 9 years old, is a time dominated by a concrete, materialistic viewpoint. The child has a sense of receiving immediate assurance from God, and material results are felt to be achieved by a process which is somewhat magical. Failure in prayer is due to naughty behaviour. God hears the prayer by physical means (e.g. he is plugged in by wires). The second stage (9 to 12 years old) is semi-magical. The child moves from an anthropomorphic to a more supernatural conception of God, so that 'God's presence' is identified with feelings of peace, happiness and confidence, rather than with a magical presence. The question of 'how do you know the prayer is effective' is answered by reference to the results of the prayer. Things happen, or can be seen to happen, as the result of the prayer; for example, people get better, people pass exams. Unanswered prayer is explained in less moralistic terms than for younger children. It is not that the pray-er has been naughty but that he or she asked for the wrong things; they were greedy or they ought to have been praying for something else. Other researchers have also distinguished between these two stages.[2]

Goldman's research was able to identify a further stage in adolescence. Here, altruistic prayer and prayers of forgiveness and confession reached their peak. The results of prayer were seen much more in terms of the spiritual results of prayer upon the person praying, perhaps mediated by the efforts or faith required. In as much as physical cures for illness were accounted for in terms of the power of prayer, God was no longer seen as intervening to cure the person but as helping doctors or scientists to find a cure. In middle or late adolescence, some young people replied that one could never be sure that an 'answer to prayer' was God's action. This was a matter of faith. By this stage 'unanswered' prayer was seen as God's refusal, for the good of his children, to fulfil some prayers. And there, Goldman implies the development of prayer is halted. The last layer of 'adult prayer' has been laid.

Research, such as that of Goldman, is valuable in demonstrating that concepts of prayer do not remain static. Layer upon layer of conceptual development, regression, and further development may be seen to take place within the different domains of prayer. We may presume that these changes continue throughout adult life, though they have never been documented as systematically as have children's prayers. As we turn to adult prayer, we shall see the importance of understanding these prior layers of prayer.

It has been known for sometime (though often forgotten) that when one passes from one developmental stage to another, the former stage is not totally replaced, but rather assimilated with later stages. It is as if additional layers were overlaid on top of the older, developmentally more primitive facets. Rather than these older elements dying out, they remain available and compete with more recently learned behaviour patterns.

Under stress, behaviour patterns learned early tend to predominate. We should expect prayer under stress to follow the same general principle. Under stress, prayer is likely to revert to the forms characteristic of earlier phases. Though people will vary in the exact form of prayer to which they revert, the kind of prayer that predominates between the ages of 7 and 9 appears to be a prime candidate. It is at this stage that people are particularly prone to pray when unhappy, and that prayer is largely self-orientated and concerned with concrete needs and wants. Prayer under stress naturally focuses on urgent personal needs. 'I hadn't prayed in ten years', exclaimed a railway worker when his train had just escaped a wreck, 'but I prayed *then.*'

Though stress gives a characteristic urgency to prayer it would be misleading to imply that it is only such prayer, or prayer that is in some way immature, that has urgency and spontaneity. George Fox, who founded the Society of Friends in the seventeenth century, will stand as an example of many religious people for whom prayer habitually had an almost compulsive quality. For many, prayer is an 'outpouring of the heart', as the Old Testament describes it in a metaphor that has recurred in descriptions of prayer. The stronger the relationship of trust to God, the more likely prayer is to arise spontaneously in times of trouble. John Bunyan put it vividly. 'Right prayer gushes from the heart when it overflows with trouble and bitterness, as blood is pressed out of the flesh by a heavy burden resting on it.'[3]

Prayer is a complex behaviour which develops through many different stages. Adult prayer is just the 'tip of the iceberg', with other earlier components being for the most part inhibited. Under stress, however, this inhibition of other aspects breaks down. There are a number of consequences of elucidating the psychological processes involved in such prayer. One is that it may help to alleviate the guilt that many people seem to feel when they find that they have prayed what seems a selfish, immature prayer. Secondly, rather than dismissing it as inauthentic, one may use it as a point of departure for more mature reflection when the stress has passed, for moments of stress can bring with them moments of disclosure and personal insight.[4] Such insights are not likely to be facilitated if prayer under stress is treated as inauthentic.

## The effects of prayer on the pray-er

Our intended emphasis on the interpretative function of prayer will focus on the effects of prayer on the person who prays rather than on its external efficacy. Those within the religious tradition who have felt uncomfortable with the apparently supernaturalist assumptions of prayer have often chosen to emphasise its effects on the pray-er. Also, many theologians have been concerned to emphasise at least that prayer is more than a method of getting external results. Thus, for example, Macquarrie contrasts forms of prayers which are 'infected by magical ideas and egotistical notions' or which try to use prayer as 'a shortcut to results that can only be achieved by toil and effort' with prayer in which we 'recognise that God and the World stand in a more intimate relation taking seriously God's immanence in the world as well as his transcendence of it ...' This, says Macquarrie, is a precondition for understanding prayer, not as bending the divine will in accordance with our desires, but rather with 'bending our will to God's will, so that the hindrances that stand in his way are removed and his good purposes for his creatures given free course'.[5] He is thus emphasising the effects of prayer on the pray-er, not at the exclusion of considering God's work in the world, but as an integral part of it.

In a major intellectual contribution to the understanding of prayer, D. Z. Phillips has taken a similar view.[6] Many philosophers have dismissed prayer as an activity in which ordinary language is stretched beyond tolerable limits, and whose efficacy cannot be demonstrated. However, taking a Wittgensteinian approach, Phillips argues that such philosophers have had a narrow a concept of 'ordinary language'. People mean something when they pray, and the task of philosophers is to determine what this is. Phillips' own view is essentially that the function of prayer lies in changing the person who prays.

In developing this point, Phillips emphasises the unique way in which language is used in prayer. Clearly it is not normally a form of dialogue, as it is rare for there to be an experience of God using language during prayer. It does not normally consist of the to-and-fro exchange of ordinary conversation. But neither is it just a soliloquy. Indeed, prayer probably could not serve its psychological functions if it were approached in this way. Our presentation of prayer as an exercise in the interpretation of experience does not imply that prayer is indistinguishable from any other reflection on experience. Central to the religious person's experience of prayer is the belief that, as William James put it, 'something is transacting'.[7] ⚡

From our psychological standpoint, we do not need to reach a conclusion on the question of whether God is really present in prayer, or whether anything external to the pray-er is achieved by prayer. However, we may note that for most people who pray, it is important for them to believe that they are not merely talking to themselves.

The view that prayer can be understood in terms of its effects on the person who prays is probably more plausible for some aspects of prayer than others. For example, it works better for confession than for petition. We will consider both in turn.

Kierkegaard provides a clear statement of the view that confession is for the benefit of the penitent rather than of God.

The person making the confession is not like a servant that gives account to his Lord for the management which is given over to him because the Lord could not manage all or be present in all places. The all-knowing One was present at each instant for which reckoning shall be made in the account ... [He] does not get to know something about the maker of the confession.[8]

Confession is not an exercise in letting God know something he did not know before. Note that there are also some human relationships in which people tell each other things they previously knew. Some expressions of love and affection are like that. Similarly, confession is not an 'informative' communication in terms of its content; there are other functions for it to fulfil.

Kierkegaard suggests what this other role might be:

the prayer does not change God, but it changes the one who offers it. It is the same with the substance of what is spoken. Not God, but you, the maker of the confession, get to know something by your act of confession.[9]

Similarly, for Macquarrie, confession is 'people's acknowledgement in the face of God, of their failure to engage themselves wholly in the way of life to which they have been called ... the prayers define and deepen the people's relation to God and promote the continual renewal of the people's dedication to him in the Holy Spirit'.[10]

Phillips needs to work harder to make out the case that petition and intercession can be understood in terms of their effects on the pray-er. Many have suggested that these forms of prayer come closest to falling into the danger of becoming selfish or magical. This is especially the case if people begin to believe that the form of words they use is somehow crucial to the efficacy of the prayer, which makes them more like an incantation than true prayer. Phillips suggests that a major difference between such magical words and true petition is that the latter has implications for the rest of the person's life. As the relationship between prayer and the rest of a person's life becomes more tenuous, so the prayer becomes suspect and the probability of superstition increases. Thus, for Phillips, prayer under stress is often not 'true prayer' since it is seldom linked with the rest of the person's life.

Phillips begins by wishing to show how prayer can change an individual, and how it is different from superstition, but he seems to conclude by saying that the effects of prayer on the pray-er constitute the *essence* of the activity. He suggests, for example that prayer of petition is best understood, not as an attempt to influence how things will go, but as an expression of devotion to God *through* the way things go. This argument contains some good points. As we will argue later in this chapter, petition has the capacity to transform a person's wishes in a helpful way. However, the weak form of the argument, that these effects are an important aspect of prayer, is rather different from the strong form that they are all there is to prayer. In siding with the strong form of the argument, Phillips may be denying the Wittgensteinian roots from which he started his analysis of prayer. For, at the outset of his influential monograph, he claimed that prayer has been much misunderstood by philosophers who have failed to take account of the contexts in which it occurs, the language-game being played when prayer is offered. One must look at whether people are using words meaningfully on their own terms, rather than imposing criteria derived from an arbitrary external criteria of 'ordinary language'.

However, Phillips himself does not keep faith with the language and concepts used about prayers of petition. People *do* talk in terms of answered and unanswered prayer. To assert that this talk is *best* understood as an expression of devotion therefore misses the mark. The language of petitionary prayer is best understood as existing within a framework in which people believe that their prayers may make a difference to what transpires. Despite the fashion for many philosophers and theologians to dismiss the interventionist model of petitions in favour of a reductionist model, a majority of people, when asked, say that there is a power of some sort that can influence the way things go, and which can itself be influenced. The paradox is that the thesis that the effects of prayer are on the one who prays may itself require that the one who prays actually believes at some level, that the thesis is false and that prayer can be answered.

Though Phillips emphasises the effects of prayer on the one who prays, he rejects the view that the kind of self knowledge arrived at in prayer is the same as that reached in other contexts. There is a limited sense in which this is clearly correct. Indeed it is doubtful whether the 'acquisition of knowledge' is at all an appropriate way to describe the cognitive changes that take place in prayer. Prayer is probably better described as the *reinterpretation* of what is in some sense already known than as an exercise in the acquisition of knowledge.

However, we can reformulate Phillips' question in terms of whether the interpretation of experience that occurs in prayer is similar to that which occurs in other contexts. The answer to this is not straight-forward. The sense of the presence of God in prayer and of his agency in the world results in the interpretation of experience reached in prayer as being different in character and content from those reached in non-religious contexts. Nevertheless, what we know in general about how experience is interpreted provides us with a valuable framework within which to understand the distinctive interpretative processes that take place in prayer. They are not so *sui generis* as to make general psychology of no relevance to understanding them.

## *Attributional aspects of religion*

The interpretation of experience is an important human activity. This is seen most clearly in the deleterious consequences that ensue when events outstrip our capacity to make sense of them. There are two kinds of situations in which this occurs. One is where events come simply too 'thick and fast', none of them perhaps particularly stressful in themselves, but together too much to cope with. In recent years there has been a great deal of psychological research on the impact of life events, and it is now clear that too many changes in a short period of time make people vulnerable both to physical and mental illness.[11] This remains true even when the individual events are in themselves of minor significance – or perhaps even positive. The reasons for this are still under investigation, as are the factors that determine how vulnerable a particular person will be to too much change, but it seems likely that a limited capacity to make sense of events is one of the key reasons why too much change can have harmful consequences.

The other situation in which events outstrip people's capacity to assimilate them is where a single, very stressful event has taken place that cannot easily or quickly be absorbed. Bereavement is one of the most common events of this kind. The process of recovery takes time, and generally follows a predictable course.[12] In the early phases there are many signs that the impact of the event has not been 'worked through'. For example, it is difficult to concentrate on anything else, because thoughts relating to the stressful event intrude. At first it may seem that little progress is being made because it is difficult to think in a clear, sequential way. Following a bereavement, people often feel too numb to think about it clearly and cannot even form a clear image of the deceased person. Thoughts about it have a repetitive, fragmented, automatic quality which in turn makes it difficult to gain any fresh perspective. However, gradually it becomes possible to think about it clearly, and there is usually a close association between this and emotional recovery.

Perhaps one of the most vivid and compelling accounts that has been given of the effort to assimilate a highly stressful event is Victor Frankl's description of coping with a concentration camp, and helping others to do the same.[13] There can hardly be any situation more appallingly stressful and debilitating, and more difficult to make sense of. Yet, in Frankl's experience, the struggle to make sense of it was, more than anything else, the key to survival. In a lecture given in 1951 on 'Group Psychotherapeutic Experiences in a Concentration Camp', Frankl describes how one day in the camp when he felt that he could scarcely endure it any longer, he imagined himself giving such a lecture. This helped to give him sufficient perspective to carry on.

Though it seems to be helpful, up to a point, to form at least some understanding (*any* understanding) of life events, the detailed content of that understanding has important psychological consequences. This is best approached in terms of the 'attribution' people make for events.[14] Psychologists have long recognised that one's reactions to a situation are determined by how one attributes the *cause* of the situation. If you fail a driving test, was it because you were having an off-day, because the examiner was in a severe mood, or because you are not a good driver? How upset you are and how quickly you apply for another test will depend on how you attribute your failure. Whenever some untoward event occurs, people tend to seek for explanations for it, and their reactions to the events depend on these explanations. A pain in the chest may be attributed to a heavy weight lifted the day before, or to an impending heart attack; a rattle in the car may be attributed to a toolbox rattling in the back or to a worn brake-shoe. The importance of attributions in determining one's reaction to these events can easily be seen. They tell the story of how we construct our personal and social world.

The pattern of attributions a person makes is related to his or her general level of self-esteem. People who have a positive regard for themselves tend to attribute their success to themselves and their failures to external factors. Those with little regard for themselves show the opposite pattern. The interest of psychologists in these processes has been increased by the role of particular patterns of attributions in leading to anxiety or depression. For the anxious patient, every noise in the house may be a burglar, every crowd may be potentially suffocating. For the depressed person, every forgotten item means they must be losing their mental powers, every time a friend doesn't smile at them means 'they must have fallen out with me'. People seldom check the validity of their attributions, with the result that a vicious spiral is set up in which greater emotional disturbance and isolation produce more maladaptive attributions and further mood disturbance. The focus of some forms of psychotherapy is to help people to identify their misattributions, to check them out, and to change them to ones that are more likely to be realistic or helpful.[15]

There is virtually no area in which one cannot see attributions at work. Why is the radio not working? Why did she smile at me? Why do I look so awful in photographs? It is almost as if the world were a silent film on which we supply our own commentary, a commentary which supplies answers to all these attributional questions.

It is not surprising, then, that peoples' religious outlooks are reflected in their patterns of attributions. However, there is no single pattern of attributions found in everyone who believes in God. It will be recalled from chapter 2 that 'committed' religious people have markedly different psychological qualities and social attitudes from those who have a merely 'consensual' religious position, and these differences are reflected in their patterns of attributions. The committed religious are likely to attribute positive events to God, whereas the consensually religious may be more likely to attribute disasters to God.[16] In general, of course, committed religious people see God as more involved in his world, more responsible for what takes place in it, than do the consensually religious.

Though the empirical investigation of attributions is a promising, recent development in the psychological study of religion, it has not yet really tackled the question of what the religious pattern of attributions consists of. Simplistically, one might regard all attributions to God as being in some senses religious attributions, but this will not really

do. For someone to attribute a disaster to the 'hand of God' may be
no more than a figure of speech for a fatalistic outlook. It is probably
in prayer that we see a religious pattern of attributions most clearly,
and the study of religious attributions could be illuminated by a greater
attention to prayer.

## Attributional processes in prayer

The pattern of attributions worked out in prayer is perhaps a more
systematic one than is found in many other contexts. For many people,
attributions of events are probably implicit and *ad hoc* rather than
consciously articulated and systematic. The negative pattern of
attributions found in depression is perhaps unusual in being relatively
systematic, but it differs from the religious one in that it seems to
emerge automatically in people who feel depressed. There is nothing
exactly like the deliberate, systematic interpretative activity found in
prayer, though the explicit attempt sometimes found in therapy to
correct maladaptive attributions is, perhaps, one of the closer
analogues.

For all that the interpretative framework applied to life events in
prayer is based on a systematic, religious world view, restraint is sometimes exercised in how fully and exhaustively this is worked out. Often,
questions about the role of God in events are raised but not answered.
To raise the question sensitises the religious person to the possible role
of God. However, from the religious point of view, there may be value
sometimes in adopting a posture of 'not knowing'. We referred in
chapter 5 to the important role of not knowing in religious insight, and
it is equally important in prayer. Apart from the theological point that
the religious person does not aspire to omniscience, there are psychological reasons why a religious interpretation of events cannot always
be pressed home. If carried too far, a religious interpretative framework becomes like an encapsulated, mechanically applied delusional
system, similar to that found in a paranoid patient who interprets
everything that happens to him suspiciously. Applied in this way,
religious interpretations of events lose the sense of imagination, play
and creativity that properly characterise what Winnicott called the
'transitional' space. As Meissner has pointed out, 'in prayer the
individual figuratively enters the transitional space where he meets
his God-representation'.[17] If the interpretative activity of prayer is to
be helpful, it needs to be undertaken with a certain lightness of touch.

Let us now consider how an attributional perspective elucidates
how prayer enables people to re-interpret events which have occurred

in their lives. Religious people are inclined to see their words and actions, not as their own, but as those of God speaking and working through them. This affects the way they approach decisions. Rather than deciding for themselves what it would be best to do, they consider what the will of God is trying to work in them, and abandon themselves to that will. When they approach life in this way, religious people may experience a certain liberation from previous limitations, and find that 'in the strength of God' they can do things that they could not have done otherwise. Equally, they may also find themselves doing things which would normally be regarded as foolish.

It is interesting to view this from the perspective of attribution theory. In psychological theory the distinction between attributions of events to internal and external factors has been especially prominent. In much of the experimental work in this field, *chance* has been taken as a typical external attribution, and *personal ability* as a typical internal attribution. As would be expected, when a person believes that his successes and failures are due to chance they do not make much impact on him and he learns little from them. Now, the religious person tends to attribute his achievements to God. Does God function here as an external attribution, a mere personification of chance?

In fact, God may function as a hybrid attribution of a unique kind; not quite internal, but not wholly external. Attributions to God show a similar pattern of functional relationships as attributions to oneself. People with positive self-regard tend selectively to attribute their successes rather than their failures to themselves. In a similar way, religious people with positive self-regard are more likely to see God as responsible for their successes than their failures. Perhaps both God and the self are salient attributions that function to accentuate the impact of successes. Failures, in contrast, tend to be ascribed to ephemeral attributions such as chance or lack of effort, which decreases their salience.

Religious people with low self-regard, who tend to be the merely consensually religious, are likely to show the opposite pattern of attributions. Both God and oneself are more likely to feature as attributes for failures, thus accentuating their impact and creating a mood of fatalism and hopelessness. Successes, in contrast, are likely to be ascribed to emphemeral attributes such as luck.

The emotional impact of attributions to God seems likely to depend on what relationship people feel they have to God. As we saw in the last chapter, this is very variable. Some people feel alienation from God; others feel almost identified with God. Between these extremes, there can be a sense of being *separate* from God, yet of being in close *relationship* with him. These possibilities seem able to explain the varying emotional impact of attributions to God. For someone who felt alienated from God, attributions to God would serve only to increase feelings of hopelessness and fatalism. For someone who felt identified with God, attributions to God would be likely to lead to arrogance and self-righteousness. However, religion can also produce a kind of detachment and humility that steers a path between hopelessness and arrogance. We suggest that this is the product of attributions to God in the person who senses he is distinct from, but closely related to, God. Such attributions seem to occupy a special place somewhere between internal and external attributions.

There is another factor that probably contributes to the religious sense of detachment and humility. This is refraining from classifying events too sharply into successes and failures. One of the distinctive features of the religious position is that, for much of the time, it leaves you not knowing whether your actions should be regarded as good or bad. There is a strong conviction that actions have implications that go far beyond their immediate and obvious consequences, often beyond what can be discerned. What may appear as a failure to the person concerned, may play an important constructive purpose in the longer-term purpose of God. Equally, what may appear to be a success may have unknown harmful consequences.

We can get some psychological handhold on this outlook from research on the perceived relationship between immediate and distant future success.[18] Where a person sees little connection between immediate achievements and distant future results, reactions to both success and failure are more muted. He is neither very eager to succeed nor is he scared of failing. The same is presumably true when only a tenuous relationship is seen between current events and God's long-term purposes. This stance makes it possible for the religious person to detach himself from the egocentric emotions frequently associated with success and failure. It is a step towards a position from which, like St Paul, he can always give thanks to God for everything (Ephesians, 5:20).

## Thanksgiving

It is indeed one of the distinctive things about giving thanks to God that He can be thanked for everything. As Phillips has pointed out, this makes it quite unlike thanking any human person. *People* are only thanked when things have gone well. If people thank God in the same way, Phillips has argued, we are committing a 'naturalistic fallacy'.

For the Christian, hope is not derived from 'things going well', but from a depth of meaningfulness which 'remains untouched by evil because it is not arrived at by an inference from it'. Meaningfulness is not determined by the balance between good and bad outcomes: 'belief in divine goodness [implies that] the meaning of life does not depend on how it goes'.[19]

This is very different from saying that evil is somehow justifiable or explicable because in the end it will have good results, or that it is part of a larger divine plan which we mortals cannot discern. Like many before and since, Phillips cannot accept that the death of a child is somehow explicable or excusable on the basis of a larger divine plan in which apparent evil is somehow good. This, he argues, would be to collude with the 'naturalistic fallacy' of making thanksgiving dependent on there being something good to be thankful for.

For Phillips, the example of Job points a different way. Job gave thanks to a supernatural God, not a natural one: 'naked came I out of my mother's womb, and naked I shall return thither: the Lord gave, and the Lord hath taken away: blessed be the name of the Lord'. The Old Testament writer does not suggest by these phrases that the events Job had suffered were really good or 'part of God's harmonious design'. He does not struggle to infer divine goodness by trying to change the nature of the evidence. Rather he comes to realise that there are some questions that do not permit explanatory answers, that there is a realm of human experience which does not invite further questions. Job could not say why the Lord gave in the first place, so he cannot say why he has taken away. Thanks to God, like hope, faith and trust in God are not dependent on 'how things go'. Rather, claims Phillips, they are an expression of a deeper understanding of the self, the world, and God. What distinguishes prayer of thanksgiving from secular attitudes to life is the kind of *acceptance* which talking to God makes possible.

However, we want to suggest that Phillips is here making too sharp an issue of whether or not there is a naturalistic basis for religious thankfulness. It is reminiscent of the too sharp distinction that has often been made between faith and knowledge. The conclusion that God exists does not flow straightforwardly from neutral observation, and neither does religious thankfulness flow straightforwardly from the nature of the events for which God is thanked. However, the other extreme is equally unattractive. Belief that God exists is not wholly unconnected with what can be observed; the religious person discovers the hand of God in creation. Equally, religious thankfulness is not heedless of the nature of events for which God is thanked in prayer.

There is here, as between faith and knowledge, a third way. The religious person can hope that his heart will be 'opencd' so that he can discern how the hand of God has been at work and give thanks for it. This will not always happen; sometimes thankfulness can be based only on trust, not on actual discernment of God's purposes. However, it is central to the psychological functions of thankfulness that the question of how God can be thanked for particular events, even for suffering and disaster, should be raised seriously. Otherwise, thankfulness will become just a mechanically applied thought system that does not help people to come to terms with actual events. Events will not be (in James Hillman's attractive term) 're-visioned'.[20]

## Confession

A religious pattern of attributions can also be found in emotional reactions to misdeeds. How these are regarded seems again to depend on what sense the religious person has of his relationship to God. With too great a sense of separation from God, awareness of God's perfection and the confession of misdeeds will only heighten the religious person's sense of worthlessness. On the other hand, with too much self-righteousness, failings may simply not be recognised and confession, if it occurs at all, will be merely mechanical. There is a widespread and well documented tendency for people to be relatively impervious to negative evidence, simply not to notice their mistakes or evidence that would disconfirm their cherished assumptions or self-confidence.[21] This pervasive cognitive bias is the foundation on which self-righteousness can easily be erected.

There is again a possibility of a third way, which recognises failings clearly but is not weighed down by them emotionally. This middle way depends on distinguishing two aspects of the attributions of misdeeds. The first is acknowledgement of one's involvement in the causal sequence, the second is the admission of self-blame ('mea culpa'). Both arise in the context of prayer. Firstly, the prayer of confession provides people with an opportunity to try and discern more clearly the various ways in which they have been part of the causal sequence leading up to a particular event. This is not just a matter of identifying blameworthy actions they hadn't previously been aware of, but of attempting to gain perspective on how events arose, to see more clearly the complex combination of factors that usually give rise to any particular event.

Secondly, there is the element of moral responsibility, rather than mere causal responsibility. There is a danger that confession, if misunderstood, will increase guilt rather than liberate people from it. In this case, it is not the prayer of confession which is the problem, but the lack of understanding of the concept of forgiveness.[22] Religious teachings have often emphasised the close linkage between feeling forgiven oneself and forgiving others. It is often portrayed as a matter of a moral duty to forgive others 'in order that we might be forgiven ourselves'. However, it can also be advocated on pragmatic grounds; not harbouring grievances helps us to feel 'free'. Seen in this latter way, the linkage between our own forgiveness and that of others is simply an emergent property of the way human psychology operates.

There has been a popular assumption since Freud that guilt consists of 'anger turned inwards towards the self', so that one will tend to observe either anger or guilt in an individual, but not both. The evidence does not bear this out. Depressed individuals, who are supposed, according to Freudian theory, to be the most clear example of anger turned inwards, tend also to be irritable and hostile. Hostility towards oneself and towards others tend to go together; reduction of one will often bring about reduction in the other. In the light of this, we may see the linkage between forgiving others and being forgiven ourselves as stating psychological facts rather than as the imposition of a rule. 'Whenever you stand praying, forgive, if you have anything against anyone; so that your Father also who is in heaven may forgive you your trespasses' (Mark, 11:25). One may see here a sensitive discernment of one of the main barriers to the experience of forgiveness; we are likely to continue to feel guilty and unforgiven by God as long as we have unresolved anger towards others.

Psychotherapy sometimes involves dealing with unresolved anger by deliberately bringing to mind and reinterpreting key events involving oneself and the other person in question. This might take the form of a role play in which patient and therapist together re-enact some past situation, changing roles occasionally, and pausing frequently to interpret what is happening. In one such situation, a young woman in her twenties who suffered from depression was discovered to have felt rejected by her mother since the age of nine. At that time, her father had died, and her mother had come to expect the little girl to suddenly grow up and cope, helping out in everything and not expressing any emotion or sign of 'weakness'. Her mother was extremely critical, and would compare her with her 'angelic' younger sister. One key situation between mother and daughter was replayed by therapist and patient, with the patient first playing the role of herself, then swapping to play the role of mother. Together

they explored what might have been said, had they not so quickly
become engaged in one of their continual arguments. The 'daughter-
as-mother' was able to experience the desperate loneliness of bereavement, of the fear that if the daughter were to break down, then she
would break down also, and of how afraid she was of not being able
to cope with such a breakdown. The 'daughter-as-herself' was able
to feel the anger and frustration of the double loss of her father and
of a loving mother, and how her anger had brought with it a sense of
being to blame which had lingered on to adult life. As she was able to
gain insight into her feeling of being rejected, and into the orgin of the
guilt and anger, she could reconstrue what had gone on between herself and her mother, opening herself to other explanations and attributions. As her feelings towards her mother resolved, so did her self-
blame, which in turn allowed her to make further progress in understanding her relationship with her mother. Being able to demonstrate
to people who feel worthless that these feelings have an identifiable
origin can be an important part of releasing them from the hold that
such feelings can have.

One of the psychological functions of confession is to help people
to gain this perspective on their lives. Such perspective will help them
to make more accurate causal attributions of potentially disturbing
events. It will also expose where actions have been blameworthy, but
because this occurs in the context of the experience of being forgiven
and of forgiving others in turn, it loosens the 'anger–guilt' knot and
frees people from its debilitating consequences.

In the last chapter we noted that relationships to people who
influence our development can serve as a model for the relationship to
God, and that there are two components in such relationships,
demands and support. The experience of confession and forgiveness
can be understood as the experience of being exposed to the gaze of
such an agent, an experience that is all the more powerful because of
the sense that God is all-knowing. The religious person finds that there
is no point in persisting with strategies of presenting themselves to
others in as favourable a light as possible; indeed there may be a sense
of relief in being liberated from the usual efforts to disguise in-
adequacies. However, there is a clear sense that God will require better
in the future, herein lies his 'demandingness'. Note here that the resolve
to do better in the future is psychologically very different from egocentric guilt about the past. The experience of standing naked before
God and being exposed to his stern demands might be overpowering
were it not balanced by the sense of being loved unreservedly by him
and of having been forgiven. The Christian sense of being forgiven is

not so much a matter of being excused for individual failings but of standing in a continuing state of having been forgiven by a loving God. It is this sense of being loved, supported and forgiven that, as in human relationships, is crucial to the stern gaze of God being experienced as liberating rather than crushing.

## *Petition*

Though we have emphasised that the effects of petition on the pray-er may depend on a belief in its external efficacy, it is with its psychological effects that we will be concerned here. Just as confession involves the experience of standing before the searching gaze of God so, in petition, religious people have the experience of standing before the gaze of God with their wishes and desires exposed. This can be a transforming process. Desires can be metamorphosed by being examined in the context of prayer.

Psychoanalysts have sometimes made a distinction between what we actually 'need' for our welfare and our more primitive, egocentric 'wishes'.[23] Petition is a context in which wishes can be transformed into needs. Also, the Christian prays not only for his own needs, but prays that God's 'will be done'. The 'thy will be done' context in which petitionary prayer is made is another factor that leads it to focus on real needs rather than mere wishes.

Psychotherapy sometimes involves a similar process of the transformation into needs of what are initially presented as wishes. A patient may come to the first session with a long list of complaints and things that they want to change. At some stage it will be necessary to look beyond such a list and to make explicit what *needs* are being expressed by it. Equally, upsetting experiences may be examined for the underlying needs that they represent. One way of doing this is to 'chase down' thoughts to their conclusions. A person may suddenly have a depressing thought or image pass through his mind, for example, that 'so-and-so didn't seem to notice me yesterday'. But why is that such a depressing thought? It is not depressing because it is so negative in itself, but because of what underlies it. If asked *why* the other person didn't notice him, the patient may reply – 'because they don't think much of me'. If asked why the other person doesn't think much of him – 'because I'm basically an unlikeable person' – and so on until one reaches some (usually extremely negative) bedrock assumption and associated basic need. Research on depressed patients has shown that there are two basic things that they are seeking to avoid: abandonment and failure.[24] The first relates to the basic need to be loved by someone, the second relates to the need to have a respected place in a social nexus.

It is characteristic of such basic needs that people are often unaware of them. However, in petitionary prayer, specific requests are allowed to come to the surface and be examined in the context of the presence of God. The experienced sternness of God can challenge primitive wishes that do not represent true needs; but the experienced lovingness of God can give people the courage to identify basic needs that they may previously not have acknowledged explicitly.[25]

In Christian teaching about petition, there has been a tendency to emphasise one or other of two extreme views. One emphasises the possibility, even desirability, of bringing before God all one's personal needs and preoccupations in their raw state. The other would emphasise that in prayer the Christian learns to desire only God and the coming of his Kingdom, and refrains from all other personal requests. Neither approach in extreme form fosters a *transformation* of personal wishes. A childlike expression of personal desires, with no consideration for how they relate to the will of God, does not lead to transformation. Equally, refraining from expressing personal wishes in prayer may simply leave such wishes as they were, and foster an artificial prayer life that is disconnected from the person's actual psychological state. As Godin has expressed it, this process of transformation is a gradual one in which the Christian faces up to 'the words of our Lord which steal slowly in among his own wishes...in a perpetually difficult symbiosis'.[26] The aim is 'mutation of attitudes' not 'suppression of the requests'. The model is the struggle of Jesus before his death; he accepted the will of the Father, but he nevertheless asked that he might live 'if it be possible'. To simulate a premature transformation of personal wishes is to evade the challenge and struggle that such a transformation presents.

The challenge presented in psychotherapy is similar, and there are comparable opportunities for evading it. It is possible to bring needs and preoccupations to therapy but to evade the task of examining them; equally it is possible to bury inconvenient issues prematurely and to simulate a new, problem-free persona. To acknowledge problematic and current needs, and to examine their significance patiently and searchingly, can lead to their transformation. However, in psychotherapy, as in petition, fundamental transformations cannot be affected quickly.

In chapter 5, we saw that religious knowing, like aesthetic or emphatic knowing, like perception under conditions of meditation, and most of all like personal insight, involves a certain distinctive *quality of attention.* This makes possible a kind of knowing in which premature attempts at symbolisation are suspended so that 'felt meanings' can emerge. It is a kind of knowing in which, in Simone Weil's phrase, we 'wait upon truth'. This attitude of mind, which depends upon a sustained and 'broad-band' quality of attention that enables connections to be seen between hitherto disparate elements, is likely to be conducive to seeing the underlying significance of immediate desires. Just as a good psychotherapist will want to enable the patient to identify what their underlying needs are so that these may be dealt with therapeutically, so an important function of the prayer of petition is to help people to become aware of their own basic needs and fears.

This is why, when reviewing the work of Goldman on the psychological development of prayer, we criticised his implicit assumption that prayer develops from immaturity (expressing specific desires) to maturity (assuming specific requests cannot be met). The psychologically transforming effects of prayer depend on holding together apparently primitive and mature features, and recognising the value of both. Unless guilt and need form part of prayer they will not be available to transformation. What passes for prayer when they are excluded may become impersonal and sterile. Prayer is a many-layered activity in which primitive layers need to be retained and interwoven with later, adult ones.

# 9

## Concepts of God

This chapter will consider the nature of religious concepts of God. Previous chapters have considered the soil from which they grow. Now we come to the characteristics of the concepts religious people use to describe the realities of the spiritual world, indeed to describe God. We will argue that the concepts that are applied to God are facets of concepts that also apply to the everyday world.

We will deliberately *not* be concerned in this chapter with the 'theistic' belief that there is a God. To the non-religious person it may appear that the most distinctive thing about religious cognition is the belief that God exists. From inside religion, this is not how it seems. The existence of God tends to be assumed as a given, rather as a scientist takes a particular research paradigm as a given framework, and tests specific hypotheses formulated within it. Similarly, for the religious person, the focus of attention is not on whether God exists but on what attributes are ascribed to him and how he is experienced. Even a cursory study of the classic religious texts shows that they are not primarily concerned to argue for the existence of God, but rather to make claims about what God is like, how he acts, and how he is experienced.

For some people, the word 'God' may be a source of problems. There are many who have broad religious sympathies, and some sense of a divine caring presence in their lives, but who are uncomfortable about calling this presence 'God'. We do not want the word to be a stumbling block to our readers. Though we will use it often in this chapter, it can be read merely as a kind of convenient short hand. Finding a name for 'God' is not only a problem for religious sceptics. There have been many Christian mystics and contemplatives who, as they have grown deeper in their knowledge of God, have grown increasingly reluctant to apply this or any other name to him. The more deeply they have come to know God, the more inadequate and misleading it has seemed to call him 'God'. Perhaps we are guilty here of talking about 'God' too glibly, though it is hard to avoid doing so. Anyhow, we would like readers who may feel uncomfortable about talking about God to know that we share some of their discomfort.

In chapter 5 we suggested that there were analogies between religious cognition and other areas of cognition such as those that arise in aesthetics and in personal insights. A parallel point can be made now about religious concepts. In all areas of psychological experience there are difficulties in finding appropriate concepts with which to describe phenomena. Physical pain, aesthetic experience, and emotional reactions, for example, are difficult to describe in ways that communicate effectively to other people. There are also second-order, theoretical problems arising from such experiential concepts, and a good deal of twentieth-century philosophy has been absorbed with a debate about whether experiential and mentalistic concepts are possible at all, and what are their rules of operation. Following our general approach, the similarities that religious concepts have with other experiential concepts will help in approaching them from a psychological standpoint.

### Double-aspect terms

An important starting point is an enquiry carried out by the social psychologist, Solomon Asch[1] into the terms used for phenomena in the psychological domain. The first striking fact is that *all* such terms have applications to physical or sensory properties too. In many cases this is very obvious, such as the description of both tastes and experiences as bitter or sweet. However, Asch found that even psychological terms which have no current physical or sensory application have one somewhere in their etymology. Asch designated such terms 'double-aspect' concepts to capture this dual reference to physical and psychological domains. The enquiry then focussed down on about 40 such concepts and studied them in eight different languages, most of which were historically independent of each other. The interesting discovery was that there were very similar physical-psychological linkages in the meanings of particular words across these different languages.[2] For example the double meaning of sweet in the Old Testament (e.g. 'Pleasant words are ... sweet to the soul', Proverbs, 16:24) is very close to its double meaning in English. Many of the central concepts in religious thought seem to have a similar double reference to physical and spiritual properties.

The concept of 'light' is a good example of a religious double-aspect concept because of the central part it has played in religious thought, not only in Christian thought but in other ancient traditions such as

Zoroastrian religion. It is also frequently reported as a feature of contemporary mystical experience.[3] The most standard use of the term light, and the one with fewest religious connotations, is to refer to the physical light that makes vision of the material world possible. Probably next most common is in the concept of intellectual light that facilitates knowledge. This is apparent in a series of terms such as 'enlightenment', 'illumination', 'clarification'. Though this is not an exclusively religious metaphor it is one that is prominent in many religions, perhaps especially in Buddhism and Christianity. Another religious use of 'light' is related to its role in making clear peoples' true moral qualities. In the presence of the divine Light, good and evil stand revealed for what they are. Then, finally, there is the description of the nature of the Godhead as light. The unapproachability of the Godhead has often been described as a kind of dazzling light. St Paul speaks of God 'whose home is in inaccessible light, whom no man has seen and no man is able to see' (1 Timothy 6:16). Even more radically, there are assertions that the nature of God is light, and that he can be experienced in no other way. Vladimir Lossky quotes St Symeon the New Theologian as saying

'God is Light and those whom he makes worthy to see Him, see Him as Light; those who receive Him receive Him as Light. For the light of His glory goes before His face, and it is impossible that He should appear otherwise than as light.'[4]

To the extent that the religious person participates in the nature of Godhead, he may also appear as light. Again, Lossky quotes a pointed anecdote in which St Seraphim of Sarov says to a disciple who is trying to understand the manifestations of the Spirit of God:

'My friend, we are both at this moment in the Spirit of God ... Why won't you look at me?'
'I can't look at you, Father ... your eyes shine like lightning, your face has become more dazzling than the sun, and it hurts my eyes to look at you.'
'Don't be afraid, at this moment you've become as bright as I have. You are also at present in the fullness of the Spirit of God; otherwise, you wouldn't be able to see me as you do see me.'[5]

To separate out these various strands of the religious meaning of light may reduce their power to some extent, as the evocativeness of the concept comes from the connections between them. It is God whose nature is light, in whose light the religious person is able to see, and by which he is himself enlightened. Light is the object, the medium, and the consequence of the contemplative vision of God.

## Metaphor

It is tempting to classify double-aspect terms such as a sweet experience, and divine light as metaphors. This would imply that it was possible to strip away the metaphors from religious thought, and to speak about God in literal language. A related notion is that, just as individual religious concepts are metaphorical, so religious thought as a whole is mythical. Again the suggestion is made that it is possible to 'demythologise' it, a programme made famous by Bultmann and much debated subsequently. However, it is not obviously correct that religious concepts are metaphorical or that religious thought is mythical. It depends on what you mean by 'metaphor' and 'myth', and there has been a good deal of confusion about this.

There is a considerable divergence of view as to what metaphor is, and what range of linguistic phenomena should be regarded as metaphorical. This has not always been brought clearly into the open, though the reason that different theorists offer conflicting theories of metaphor seems to be at least partly that they have different phenomena in mind. Cassirer, in *Language and Myth*,[6] made a distinction between a narrow sense of metaphor, which involves the conscious denotation of one thought content by another, and radical metaphor, in which the two ideas involved are not clearly distinguished. Asch's double-aspect terms are an example of the latter. In a recent major work on *Metaphor and Religious Language*,[7] Soskice takes a strict view of metaphor that is reminiscent of Cassier's narrow concept. She defines metaphor as 'that figure of speech whereby we speak about one thing in terms which are seen to be suggestive of another'. She rejects the idea that *words* are metaphorical in any general sense. Rather it is speakers and hearers who *use* words metaphorically. The notion that metaphorical words have two meanings is another that she rejects. Metaphorical uses of words have about them a 'tension' that reflects the fact that the metaphorical use has not yet been lexicalised (i.e. come to be an established meaning of the kind that would justify a dictionary entry). All this makes clear that, on these strict criteria, double-aspect terms are not metaphors.

One implication of Soskice's strict definition of metaphor proper is that it is a phenomenon that has rather little place in religious thought and writing, though she does not seem to have seen this implication clearly and there is consequently a curious disjunction between the sections of her book dealing with the theory of metaphor and the sections dealing with religious language. Clearly, *images* abound in religious thought, but they are so well established there is none of the tension about their religious use that she requires for metaphor. Their religious use has become lexicalised.

The confusion about whether or not classic religious concepts should be regarded as metaphors outcrops in an interesting way in a recent and excellent book on biblical language by George Caird.[8] He cites passages from both John Robinson and Eric Mascal in which they claim that the description of the Church as the body of Christ is a literal truth. Caird regards this as palpably absurd, because to him it is clear that this is a metaphorical use of 'body'. However, it is such an established use of the term 'body' that it no longer has the tension associated with an extended use of a word that Soskise takes as one of the characteristics of a strict metaphor. Also the use of the term 'body' for an institution, as in 'body politic' is a well established, secondary lexical usage of the word 'body'. The application of the word 'body' in this sense to the Church is a quite straightforward, unmetaphorical one. In part, it is just a point of terminology how strictly metaphor is to be defined, and whether or not religious concepts such as 'light' or 'body' fall within it. Caird does not dispute the fact that with many religious metaphors we are no longer aware of the duality of meaning.

If religious concepts like 'light' and 'body' are not metaphors on strict criteria, what are they? One common answer is that they are 'dead' metaphors. It is often assumed that all such words must have begun as living metaphors, i.e. metaphors in Soskise's strict sense. Someone at sometime took a word that previously had only an ordinary literal usage and employed it in a novel, extended way to refer to something religious or experiential. It is assumed that this new metaphor 'caught on', and eventually became an established term in the religious or experiential domains. This etymological thesis is seldom stated so baldly, but it seems to be implicit in much that is written about religious and experiential terms. Indeed, it is a widely held theory about how all established or 'dead' metaphors originated. However, the grounds for holding this view are very weak. It is not just that there is no direct evidence but that, as Barfield[9] has argued, such evidence as is available actually points against it. There are two main lines of circumstantial evidence. One is that the study of etymology indicates that the further back in time you go, the more 'metaphorical' or symbolic language is found to be. Why then assume that there is an earlier, undiscovered stage in the use of words when they were used literally? The other relevant consideration is that, as Asch discovered, a great many of the same double-aspect terms appear in historically independent languages. If their origin is in terms of adventitious creation of metaphor this seems a coincidence that it is difficult to credit.

The prevalence of the view that religious concepts have a metaphorical origin is probably related less to positive support for it than to the problem of entertaining a plausible alternative. However, the alternative that Cassier, Barfield and others have offered deserves serious consideration. It begins from the assumption that there have been historical changes in human consciousness. Some of the grounds for assuming recent changes were presented briefly in chapter 7. The general assumption of genetic psychologists[10] has been that human development has been accompanied by increasing differentiation between subject and object, i.e. between subjective experience and the material world. This suggests a possible alternative view of the origin of double-aspect terms. Perhaps it was not that terms were extended metaphorically from material to experiential applications, but that *they were applied to both domains from the outset because no clear differentiation was made between them.*

In talking of the divine light, the religious person is perhaps not merely using a figure of speech, not projecting the connotations of a visual frame of reference on to a quality of the Godhead. Perhaps light was originally seen as a double-aspect reality that required a double-aspect term to refer to it, in which case the religious concept of light would not be an adventitious metaphor but would reflect an awareness of the double-aspect nature of light. It is not our purpose here to argue whether or not particular double-aspect terms originated as metaphors or not, but that there is a coherent theory of their non-metaphorical origin that deserves to be seriously considered.

Changes in the use of metaphor can be traced through the Old Testament. Ferré[11] has suggested that much apparently figurative language in the Old Testament antedates any distinction between literal and metaphorical language. He makes a distinction between what he regards as this unselfconscious use of metaphor that can be found, for example, in the prophets and the more contrived figurative language of apocalyptic literature such as the book of Daniel. However, Caird[12] suggests that if there ever existed a 'mythopoeic' mind that grasped everything in a unitary act of perception, 'it already lay far in the past before the earliest document of the Old Testament was written', though he also recognises changes in the use of myth within the Old Testament period. For example, he suggests that deliberate, pragmatic uses of myth to argue for a particular religious interpretation of events belong exclusively to the exilic or post-exilic period.

Though earlier forms of consciousness may have been better adapted to the discovery of double-aspect realities than contemporary consciousness, the capacity for this has not been altogether lost. We made the point in an earlier chapter that one of the cognitive results of the relaxed mode of consciousness induced by meditation techniques is that it facilitates 'parallel processing' in which several strands of thought can be attended to simultaneously. This seems likely to increase sensitivity to double-aspect phenomena. One of the features of mystical experience in William James'[13] classic description is that it produces a sense of the unity and relatedness of things. This sense of relatedness also seems likely to arise out of a kind of thinking that is organised in parallel processes. Someone who is thinking in multiple strands of thought will find it possible to grasp the inter-relatedness of all things in a way that will be much more difficult for sequential thinking.

Whether figurative religious language is formulated as double-aspect terminology, or as metaphor in the strict sense proposed by Soskice, it is inappropriate to require that it be translated into literal language. C.S. Lewis[14] has made a distinction that is helpful here between masters' and pupils' metaphors. In the former case the metaphor is introduced to help to explain an idea that could perfectly well be formulated in other terms; in the latter the metaphor is the only way of expressing the idea and is, for the time being at least, indispensable to it. Another relevant concept is Black's[15] notion of the degree of 'emphasis' that a metaphor has, which refers to its reducibility to literal language.

There is never any difficulty in re-casting masters' metaphors in literal language. However, contrary to what is often assumed, this is not true of all metaphors. Strong claims have sometimes been made[16] that (a) if metaphors cannot be reduced to literal statements they are devoid of cognitive meaning and (b) because many religious metaphors cannot be so reduced they are meaningless. However, as Soskise[17] correctly argues there is no inherent virtue in literal language, and it is not the only form of meaningful language. Metaphorical statements can be explicated in other ways apart from being reduced to literal statements, and the fact that they are capable of explication is sufficient to save them from the charge of meaninglessness.

If many religious terms can be properly regarded as double-aspect terms that refer to double-aspect realities, the request for reduction to literal statements is particularly inappropriate. It is especially puzzling that some Christians appear to regard literal interpretations of religious doctrines as the only valid ones, and insist that only those who accept doctrine at a literal level are true believers. Embedded in this position is a kind of materialism that is unwilling to give proper weight to spiritual realities. It is strange to find such a line of thought deeply embedded in some traditions of religious thinking.

### Prototypicality

Another conspicuous feature of many religious symbols is their prototypicality. It is not just that God is one member of the class of entities characterised by light. He *is* light. For the Christian, God is the source of all light. He is perfect light, the prototype of all light-filled beings. Prototypicality is also nicely illustrated by several of the 'I ams' of St John's Gospel, such as 'I am the Good Shepherd.' The range of meanings of 'good' here includes both 'prototypical' and 'perfect'.

For a long period, psychologists approached the formation of concepts in terms of a theory of abstraction by which a series of instances are classified in categories, and the common features abstracted to arrive at the general concept. This theory runs into a number of difficulties as an exhaustive account of how class concepts are formed, but the one that is relevant here follows from an insight of Wittgenstein. He realised that there is frequently disagreement over the borderline cases in conceptual categories, but agreement over the paradigmatic exemplifications of the concept. There may indeed be a sufficient number and diversity of problematic borderline cases to make it impossible to define a concept in terms of features shared by all, or even most, exemplifications of the concept. What seems to happen instead is that people define a concept in terms of its exemplars.

Thus, classical religious symbolic concepts like the good shepherd are making use of a style of thinking in terms of prototypes that is very common. The prototype of a 'shepherd' is not based on an abstraction of the characteristics that actual shepherds have in common, but on a more intuitive concept of the 'paradigmatic' shepherd.

The experimental investigation of the use of prototypical instances in conceptual thinking has become a fruitful area of psychological research. One interesting product has been a renewed emphasis on non-analytical processes in conceptual thinking. People typically do not think through all the relevant information in an analytical fashion when making a judgement, but use short-cut heuristics that are often based on prototypical instances. This sometimes results in important information being ignored. For example, if you are making a prediction about which of several courses of action a person will take, you would probably do it on the basis of matching the person concerned to concepts of the prototypical person who takes each course of action. Other relevant factors, especially quantitative factors, like the statistical probability of each course of action being followed, may be ignored. The link between thinking in terms of prototypes and an intuitive mode of cognition also applies to religious thinking. We pointed out in chapter 5 that the cognitive mode induced by meditation has important non-analytical features. This is an additional reason why religious thinking finds prototypical concepts such as the good shepherd congenial.

Though part of the meaning of 'good shepherd' is captured by 'prototypical shepherd', there are other aspects to its meaning. It also means 'ideal shepherd'. Actually this is a more modest extension than might appear, because there are many classes of things where paradigmatic exemplifications are rare and the vast majority of exemplifications are 'flawed' cases at the boundary of the concept. Thus, for example, it is rare for a handmade piece of pottery to be a perfect shape. Because of this, many concepts are better defined in terms of rare ideal exemplifications than in terms of commonly found cases.

The study of ideal types has an established place in the methodology of the social sciences. A particular phenomenon is explained by relating it to the ideal type of which it is an imperfect exemplification. It was the method used by Goethe in his classical studies of plant morphology to which we referred in chapter 5 which led to his idea of the archetypal plant of which all actual plants are exemplifications undergoing metamorphosis. Goethe's views are not a mere historical curiosity. Those contemporary biologists who maintain a field theory of organisms,[18] hold that the growth of an organism can only be explained in terms of some kind of a pre-existing template of the fully developed organism to which it increasingly approximates during growth. Such a template notion, though species-specific, has some similarities to Goethe's notion of the plant archetype.

Jungian psychology assumes something similar in the area of person perception by introducing the notion of an archetype (the 'great mother', the 'puer aeternus' etc.) that is projected on to particular people who approximate the archetype sufficiently well to be capable, at least for a time, of offering a screen onto which it can be projected. Though there are similarities between the views of Goethe and Jung here, they differ in where they locate the reality of the archetype, Jung seeing it as primarily in the psyche and Goethe seeing it primarily as surrounding the material plant. However, there may in the end be no necessary disjunction between the two views.

It will be obvious how prevalent such ideal-type concepts are in religious thinking. For example, one of the most central ideas in Christianity is that individual men and women are all flawed exemplifications of the ideal prototype of the 'anthropos'. From this point of view, part of the significance of the Christ is as a uniquely perfect exemplification of the class of men. There is a sense in which, for the Christian, the concept of the ideal prototype of man is involved in his understanding of all particular men. There is at least an analogy to be drawn between this and Jung's view of how the archetypes of the psyche are involved in person perception and Goethe's view of how the idea of the archetypal plant is involved in the manifestation of particular plants. The Christian seeks to cultivate a sense of how each man and woman would be if he or she were not 'flawed', and by living with this concept to help the people concerned to develop towards a fuller exemplification of it.

## *Myth and sacrament*

Religious 'myth' raises issues that parallel those relating to religious metaphor. It is commonplace to suggest that religious beliefs are 'mythical' rather than factual. Yet this raises more questions than it answers, because there is such a diversity of views as to what a 'myth' is. One of the problems with the term is that it is used by theologians and philosophers in a technical sense that differs from its mainstream meaning of a 'purely fictitious narrative' (as the OED puts it). One thing that is generally *not* being said when it is suggested that religious beliefs are mythical is that they are purely fictitious. It is generally being suggested they are in some sense true, but that their truth is symbolic rather than literal or factual.

However, at this point divergences open up about the nature of mythical truth. John Hick[19] suggests that the truth of a myth is not literal but 'is a kind of practical truth consisting in the appropriateness of the attitude it evokes'. Other theologians have had a different view of myth. Bultmann[20] in proposing his programme of demythologisation, defined myth as 'the use of imagery to express the other world in terms of this world and the divine in terms of human life, the other side in terms of this side'. On this view, myths do not just induce 'appropriate' responses, they say something correct about the 'other side', but use the language of 'this side' to convey it. But what exactly are these 'sides'? The problem with this definition of myth is that it seems itself to be rather mythological. Certainly, talk of the 'other side' does not seem to be literal talk. This seems a rather crucial failure for Bultmann's programme of demythologisation. If he hopes to speak in literal, non-mythological terms about the 'other side' it would make a useful start to say in literal language what he means by this 'other side'. His failure to do so does not inspire confidence in his programme.

But what *could* this 'other side' be? There are two main candidates. One would be the 'supernatural' world. However, this does not appear to be what Bultmann had in mind. For no very good reason (except that it is what modern man generally thinks) he seems to have held the view that there is no supernatural world. This leaves him an existentialist interpretation of the 'other side' as an inner world, apparently the interpretation he favoured. If religious statements were demythologised, they would apparently be about human experience, about the depths of the human psyche. Readers might assume that this would be an attractive programme to psychologists writing about religion, but this is not necessarily the case. Firstly, the reasons offered by demythologising theologians for abandoning the concept of the supernatural are surprisingly derivative. Bultmann simply takes it for granted that modern science has made it impossible to talk of the supernatural. However, modern science is far from having arrived at a fixed point, and it is too soon to say whether or not it will be possible to arrive at a paradigm that integrates 'natural' and 'supernatural' phenomena (in the way that psychosomatic medicine integrates physical and psychological phenomena). The fact that the current scientific paradigm is not of this kind says nothing at all about what is actually true. Secondly, there is no way of describing the human psyche except by the use of figurative or double-aspect language. It is thus doubtful whether translating religious statements into psychological statements would make them any more 'literal'.

The choice of whether religious statements should be taken as referring to existential or supernatural realities may in the end prove to be misleading. Jung's concept of the 'collective unconscious' points the way to a possible integration of the two. There may be a domain that is 'inner' in the sense of being at the root of human experience, but is also collective and objective rather than merely private and personal. There is not yet agreement as to whether or not there is such a domain. In the meantime it may be prudent to question whether it is appropriate to say that religious statements must refer to *either* supernatural *or* existential realities.

A view of myth that seems more satisfactory than that held by theologians arguing either for or against demythologisation is again that of Cassirer.[21] He seeks to steer a path between two views of myth that he regards as equally unsatisfactory. He is firm in rejecting the view that myth is an 'invented' phenomenon, whose genesis can be explained in terms of laws of association. However, Cassirer is no happier with the metaphysical view that sees myth as reflecting the 'unity of the absolute'. This he sees as of little use in characterising the form and nature of mythical thinking, which is the aspect that interested him. Unlike both the genetic and metaphysical approaches, he advocates what can be termed a non-reductionist view of myth. One of his key themes is that myth identifies the part with the whole, and the word with the reality it denotes. One could add that myth is often concerned with prototypical events. For example, the Christian myth of the Fall is presented as the root and quintessence of a multiplicity of individual human failings.

Similar issues are raised in connection with sacramental thinking, especially the symbolism of the Christian Communion. Here again there has been a tendency for views about the relationship between the bread and wine, and the body and blood of Christ, to dichotomise into those that, with a crude literalism, equate the two, and those that regard the former as *merely* a symbol of the latter. Neither view has proved satisfactory. The Communion is not a mere piece of dramatic allegory, and can no more be reduced to a set of literal statements that 'unpack' the allegory than can radical double-aspect concepts such as divine Light. Jung in an essay on the psychology of the symbolism of the Mass[22] documents the way in which the basic elements of the Communion parallel those of other religious rituals, thus making the point that we are dealing not with a *contrived* metaphor but with the *discovery* of a piece of radical symbolism about the everyday becoming holy through an act of sacrifice.

But on the other hand, neither is the sacramental thinking of Christianity a mere outcropping of primitive mythical thinking that would make no distinction at all between the bread and Christ's body. Cassirer explored the tension between mythical and sacramental thinking in a way that is relevant here. In religious thinking, unlike myth, there is a tension between the symbol and the symbolised that is never resolved. They are neither identified nor finally separated. The history of religion is in part the story of the injection into mythical thinking 'of an alien tension ... in order to disintegrate and destroy it from within'.[23] As Cassirer points out, this process can be traced through the Hebrew prophets, and the prohibition of idolatory can be understood in these terms. However, if the process of dissolution were to go too far, religion would degenerate into aesthetics, in which the symbol was recognised as such with no notion that it was anything more. The subtlety of this inherent tension in religion seems to have been missed by many of those who have argued for or against demythologization, but it is essential to a proper understanding of the issues. Religious myth maintains this tension. It inhabits a domain in which questions of interpretation can properly be raised, but a complete literal rendering is never possible.

### Animism: Primitive and Mature

Religious thinking is often concerned with *processes* (activities, transformations, etc.) or with *relations* between things, seldom with a static view of discrete entities.[24] This is especially true of primitive religious thinking. The Gods and the Spirit were known more through their actions than through their qualities. There is also a strong tendency to interpret natural events (wind, rain, etc.) and human events (death, victory in battle, etc.) as the actions of the spirit world. The phrase 'Act of God' is a survival of this thinking.

There is a sense in which the Communion has provided a stage on which different styles of thinking about processes and relations have been argued out. The Communion is concerned with the relationship between two natural things (bread and wine) and two 'spiritual' things (the body and blood of Christ), and with the process by which the latter take on the properties of the former. The Christian sees divine involvement in the metamorphosis of the bread and wine in the Communion; there is said to be a sense in which Christ is the celebrant at every Mass. The bread and wine are held to take on the living powers of Christ's body and blood. This could be seen as a specific case of animistic thinking, which in its more primitive and unrestrained manifestations is inclined to see everything as alive and imbued with the spirit world. However, there are important distinctions to be made between primitive animism and mature thinking about spiritual processes.

It has been suggested that one of the reasons why religious thinking is often linked to activities and relations is that these are more difficult to perceive accurately than are discrete objects. They leave more scope for the intrusion of magical thinking. However, there is also a mature animism which occurs despite the fact that there is no lack of capacity for other modes of thought. Animistic thinking has been shown to have very different meanings for children and adults.[25] There is a distinction between the primitive, undifferentiated perceptual style of the child and the mature anthropomorphism of the adult, which presupposes differentiation of the personal and impersonal but voluntarily chooses to transcend it. The adult begins from a capacity to differentiate discrete entities, but may choose to use his imagination to discern processes and relationships that are superficially similar to those found in primitive, undifferentiated perception.

Similar points emerged from an empirical study of animistic thinking in University students, in which it was found that animistic thinking is more common among intelligent, civilised adults than is commonly supposed.[26] But these adults showed a capacity to think *either* in animistic *or* non-animistic ways as a matter of choice. They could make accurate, literal distinctions between living and non-living objects, but they could also give examples of times when they had attributed life to objects not normally regarded as living. Prized possessions and photographs, for example, can be treated as if they were living. Whereas primitive thinking instinctively sees the natural world as inhabited by spirits influencing man, animistic thinking in modern man is deliberate and conscious. Primitive man saw the spirit world as speaking to him through nature. In modern religious man, it is more as though an inner sense of life is projected outwards. This historical change in the 'direction' of thinking was discussed in chapter 7.

### Children's understanding of religious metaphors

Differences between primitive and mature animism are paralleled in differences between how children and adults understand metaphor. There is no doubt that clear developmental trends can be discerned in children's reactions to metaphor. However, there has been disagreement about what stage in this development should be taken as indicating that children understand a particular metaphor. One fact which has emerged very clearly is that the ability to *explain* metaphors comes later than the ability to *use* them, though there may be nothing distinctive to metaphor about this. The same is probably true of literal sentences. Also, the fact that a child cannot explain a metaphor doesn't necessarily mean that he doesn't understand it. He may, for example, understand the sense in which God is light, without being able to explain it. Perhaps the idea that you can't be said to understand a metaphor until you can explain it is a hangover from the discredited idea that every metaphorical statement can be replaced by a literal statement.

Though children clearly understand metaphors before they can explain them, there may nevertheless be significant differences between the use of metaphors before and after the acquisition of the capacity to explain them. It has been suggested[27] that 'what remains as connotative relationship in adults may in many cases start as a denotative non-differentiation'. To adapt the terminology we used above about how metaphors are comprehended, children may be more likely to perceive a metaphor through fusion of its components; adults may be more likely to scan for resemblances between two distinguished things.

These issues can be brought into sharper focus by examining the thorough empirical study of the development of religious thinking in children carried out by Goldman, to which we referred in chapter two and again in the last chapter. One of the stories Goldman used was Moses' perception of a burning bush as God. This is closely related to the 'metaphorical' concept of God as dazzling light. The story was evidently very puzzling to the younger children, who could only offer crude accounts of how it was that the bush appeared to burn, but did not burn up. Above the age of about 12, when children move into the period of what Piaget has called formal operational thinking, some children were able to grasp that Moses might have seen a fire-like manifestation of Divine energy that did not actually burn (e.g. 'It might not be flames, but something like flames, to attract Moses to go over there' or 'It was a flame of goodness, not a burning flame ... God put it there.' 'There are flames of holiness everywhere, but he made Moses see this one. Usually they are unseen.'). The interpretation of other children in this age group, while departing from the crude notions of younger children, showed little grasp of the double-aspect concept of the divine Light involved here (e.g. 'It might have been the sun in a certain direction making it look like flames' or 'There wasn't really a fire. It was a mirage in Moses' thought.').

Though these strands appear to be equally represented in the examples Goldman gives of the thinking of children over about 12, this is not how he summarises his findings. Rather he suggests that there is a progression from ideas about God's personal intervention in the physical world to a later stage where 'the explanations become entirely non-physical, where the light or flame is not real and merely symbolises the presence of God, this latter giving way to the experience largely based upon an internal encounter with God, as it were, in Moses' mind'. The problem here is that Goldman appears to think that the symbol of burning can only be taken *either* in a crudely literal, magical, materialistic way *or* alternatively in a merely symbolic or psychological way. The latter is regarded as the more advanced understanding of the event. Yet some of the *merely* symbolic interpretations of the older children might be seen as a move even further away from a grasp of the divine energy that transcends and encompasses both physical and spiritual light, compared with the unelaborated ideas of some young children (e.g. 'God made it happen').

Similar points about the irreducible character of radical religious metaphors could have been made with a great variety of examples. The comprehension of religious parables such as those of Jesus raise similar issues. There has been a widespread tendency to treat these as stories that make points in a picturesque way that could equally have been made in a literal way. However, a similar case can be made out for the irreducibility of the language of parables.[28]

## Comprehension of metaphors

How metaphors are understood is an unresolved issue that is currently attracting a lot of interest from psychologists.[29] Metaphorical statements pose a problem for theories of language comprehension. The challenge is to explain how and why they are not *mis*understood. If a metaphorical sentence were treated as though it were a literal sentence, the correct meaning would not be conveyed. If a preacher says that Christians are called to be soldiers, he is not urging them to enlist in the national army, though this is what a literal reading would suggest.

There are basically two kinds of solution to this problem. One is to propose that people have a capacity to differentiate metaphorical sentences from literal ones. It is not difficult in principle to see how this might be done. Taking Soskice's point about the internal tension in a metaphorical sentence, the essential task would be to monitor whether this tension was present and, if so, to abort the normal process by which literal sentences are understood. The other solution is a more radical one and involves abandoning altogether the notion of 'literal meaning' of a sentence as the vehicle of sentence comprehension.[30] According to this latter view, which has recently been gaining ground, the essential task for a speaker when listening to a sentence is to discern the illocutionary force of a sentence (i.e. what a sentence means or implies in its context). Many sentences, even literal sentences, can be used in a variety of different ways. Consequently trying to discern *the* literal meaning of a sentence is often not particularly helpful in understanding what is meant by it in a particular context.

One of the reasons for preferring this latter solution is that the first one has difficulty in handling the problems posed by the comprehension of sentences involving double-aspect terms. Take the sentence 'John is a cold person.' The use of 'cold' as meaning unfriendly in this sentence is so ubiquitous that the sentence contains no inherent tension. If, therefore, we were scanning for signs of metaphorical usage we might well fail to pick up that this sentence was a metaphorical one. Indeed, in a strict sense, it is not metaphorical. Similar problems arise with understanding many sentences involving symbolic religious concepts such as 'God is light'. Again, the double-aspect use is so established that on many criteria it would not be singled out as a metaphorical sentence. The task of understanding what is meant by a sentence is probably essentially the same whether it is literal or metaphorical. The primary task is to find an interpretation of the sentence which is coherent. To do this, the listener selects from the network of meanings and associations of each word those that can find a place in an integrated interpretation of the sentence.

With sentences in which a key word is used figuratively, what is required is not just selecting its 'literal' or its 'metaphorical' meaning according to which will fit best in the context. Neither, of course, is it a matter of altogether failing to distinguish the different facets of meaning of double-aspect terms such as 'light'. What is required is a middle way. It is rather like the middle way in understanding the myth and sacrament that neither completely identifies the two facets (e.g. 'bread' and 'body') nor separates them so sharply that one is treated as a *mere* symbol of the other. It is also like the mature animism that can make distinctions when desired, but chooses not to. Essentially the same point is made in the Athanasian Creed about the three persons of the Trinity when it speaks of neither 'confounding the persons' nor 'dividing the substance'.

The interpretation of psychological sentences like 'John is a cold person' and religious sentences like 'God is Light' needs to be based on first distinguishing the different facets of meaning of the terms concerned ('cold' and 'light') but then, secondly, drawing on the richness of *both* facets of their meanings in as far as they can be integrated into a coherent formulation of the sentence. The interpretation of metaphorical sentences, to borrow some terminology from current psychological work on metaphor[31] depends, not so much on scanning back and forth between the juxtaposed meanings, but on fusing the two meanings into a single interpretation of how the metaphor is used in a particular sentence. It is analogous to looking at a modern painting in which unexpected things are juxtaposed. Responding to such a painting involves drawing together the relevant aspects of the meaning and significance of each separate object and blending them together in a single coherent vision of the painting.

## Doctrinal concepts

It might be objected that the religious concepts that have been chosen for discussion so far in this chapter are highly selected ones that suit a psychological approach, and that there are other kinds of religious concepts for which it is harder to give a psychological account. The more 'doctrinal' concepts, such as the Christian concept of the Trinity, might be cited as the kind of religious concept that lend themselves to a psychological approach less readily.

Gary Gutting, in a recent book[32] has drawn an explicit distinction between what he has called the 'core' and 'outer belt' of religion, deriving these terms from a parallel distinction that is sometimes made between the 'hard core' and 'protective belt' of scientific research programmes. The core of religious belief is, he suggests, the awareness of a divine, loving presence. The outer belt of religious belief includes the more doctrinal commitments that form the content of religious creeds. These two kinds of religious ideas differ in their closeness to experience. It might be pointed out that the kind of double-aspect concepts of the qualities of God, such as the idea that God is light, are concepts that are closer to the experiential core of religion, but that as one moves to the more doctrinal concepts of the outer belt, psychology is less relevant.

There is much plausibility in this point, but there is a danger of admitting too readily that the more doctrinal religious ideas are divorced from experience. It is probably correct that there are more people who have an experiential basis for the idea that God loves them and cares for them than for the idea that God is a Trinity. However, we want to suggest that this is not a necessary state of affairs. The experiential basis and psychological significance of the doctrine of God as Trinity may be obscure, but we want to indicate how this kind of 'doctrinal' concept can have a psychological aspect.

The key to seeing this possibility is to grasp that the Trinity is not just an abstract metaphysical formulation about a transcendent God, but potentially a characterisation of aspects of everyday experience. From a Christian standpoint, it would be expected that if the nature of God is Trinitarian, this would be reflected in creation (in man and in the natural world). This implies the possibility of 'discovering' the Trinitarian nature of God through its reflection in everyday experience. There is, in fact, a long tradition of seeing the Trinity reflected in man and nature, as well as in the transcendent God. Augustine, in his *Confessions*,[33] drew an analogy between Being, Intellect and Will in man and the three persons of the Trinity. Many others have elaborated similar conceptions. For example, in the thirteenth century Ramon Lull based his 'art of memory' on the Trinity.[34] Much more recently, Jung has drawn a parallel between Trinity and the structure of the psyche, though his inclusion of the Devil as well in a 'quaternity' is somewhat heterodox.[35]

If the Trinity is an idea about God that is potentially discoverable on the basis of psychological experience, then of course it would not be expected to be unique to a single religion. This might seem a strong objection to the idea that the Trinity can potentially have a basis in experience. However, the concept of the Trinity may be less unique to Christianity than is often supposed. Raimundo Panikkar in his book, *The Trinity and the Religious Experience of Man*[36] has argued that the essentials of the Trinitarian idea are found much more widely in thinking about God. God is unknowable source (brahman); God is a person, a mediator to whom man can relate; God is an imminent, indwelling Spirit with whom man can unite (atman). These are concepts of God that go much wider than Christianity.

The intellectual puzzle raised by the Trinitarian concept of God is how God can be *both* one *and* three. It was with this conundrum that the Athanasian Creed grappled in the fourth century. Again, the pattern of formal relationships implicit in the Trinity is not unique to it. Margaret Masterman[37] has argued that similar formal relationships are used in quantum mechanisms and have been formalised mathematically in Boolean algebra. She concludes that 'the Early Greek Fathers were feeling after a very general way of thinking, which, centuries after − other men have mathematised, and which ... may be fundamental to thinking about the foundations of the Universe itself'.

To pursue the potential psychological basis of the Trinity any further would become an exercise in theology rather than psychology. Clearly, it is a more complex religious concept than ideas such as God as Light or as Love. If it arises from experience at all it may only be as the distillation, after deep reflection, of a breadth of experience. However, the possibility of discovering the Trinitarian relationships in both nature and God cannot be dismissed. The Trinity may be more similar than would initially be supposed to double-aspect concepts such as light. The distinction between 'core' and 'outer belt' religious concepts may not be a qualitative one, but only reflect a difference in degree of complexity.

## Resonance

Finally, we will consider some related issues that arise in the *use* of symbolic religious language. The richness or meaningfulness of metaphors has been said to depend on their network of associations,[38] and religious 'metaphors' often involve a network of associations that is particularly rich. In addition, religious concepts frequently operate in various different frames of reference.[39] For example, the concept of the Messiah was a very resonant one for the Jews, and this was partly due to the fact that it had a central place in their political aspirations as well as in their religious life. The history of the use of religious concepts represents a constant reworking and enrichment of their network of associations. It is a use of language that Soskice[40] has aptly described as 'emblematic' rather than metaphorical. Central religious symbols are reworked in gloss upon gloss, weaving a complex of meanings that becomes almost inexhaustible.

Again, a parallel with how metaphors are elaborated and reworked in psychotherapy will illuminate how religious metaphors can be reworked. Important moments of insight in psychotherapy are often associated with the use of metaphorical language, though this can take several different forms. Sometimes new metaphors are created. At other times established metaphors are re-worked in a rich, personal way, or an attempt is made to explicate them as far as possible in literal language.

A good example comes from psychotherapy of a patient who felt a sense of weakness and inadequacy as a person.[41] He was also a keen athlete, and this provided him with a rich network of associations for the double-aspect metaphor of strength (physical strength/strength of character) that played a key role in his psychotherapy. Though he used a variety of other metaphors, this is one that he introduced into the therapy himself and which had the unique property of showing a steady increase in usage over time. The first time this metaphor was introduced, the patient was describing how he became angry with his girl friend when she asked him if he could carry some packages. Reflecting on this, he suggested that it was as though he was saying 'Why are you questioning me? I'm strong enough to carry them. Why do you need to ask me whether I can carry them?' Though the double-aspect concept of strength is old and ubiquitous, there is a sense here of the patient using it to grope towards an understanding of a specific application of the metaphor that he had not yet fully grasped. Gradually over the therapy, the connection between his athletic prowess and his sense of personal inadequacy was grasped more consciously.

Generalising about how metaphor is used in psychotherapy, Gendlin[42] has suggested that it often passes through four stages. Firstly there is a straining inward to grasp some aspect of personal experience of which one had previously hardly been aware. Next comes a stage of 'unfolding' when implicit feelings are made explicit. Thirdly, there is a phase of elaboration when relevant associations flood into consciousness. Finally, these are distilled in a way that can influence how the patient understands himself and will respond to future experiences. Perhaps religious knowing passes through similar stages. Consider, for example, the age-old metaphor of God as love. The root of a new experience of this metaphor would be when a person turns inward, experiences the sense of being loved by God, and makes this feeling explicit. Dwelling on this experience, it can bring a wide range of associations into consciousness, drawing on anything relevant in the person's experience both of God and of love. As a result the metaphor of God as a love will be enriched for that person and acquire a new numinosity. New understandings may be formulated which will stay with the person and affect how he lives his life. Insight in psychotherapy usually begins by seeing *linkages* (such as that between personal strength and strength of character). It is only much later that the patient is able to develop these and integrate them into anything approaching a coherent formulation of the nature of his psychological problems. Doctrinal concepts such as the Trinity are the religious equivalents of such integrative formulations of personal insights.

This process of explicating and constantly reworking religious symbols requires considerable mental effort. In the absence of such effort, traditional religious symbols tend to become nothing more than dead metaphors. There are probably many signs, in the way a religious speaker uses religious symbols, of whether or not this effort is being made. If it is, there are likely to be novel embellishments on religious symbols within their traditional figurative domains. There may well also be attempts at partial explication in literal statements, though such explication will never achieve completeness. There will probably also be paralinguistic cues which indicate whether religious symbols have become mere dead metaphors. In psychotherapy, there is a characteristic tone of voice associated with useful self-exploration that differs from the one used in other parts of the session.[43] The difference in tone of voice is analogous to that between reading and spontaneous speech. The voice used in spoken religious languages also often betrays whether or not the speaker is making the cognitive effort to rework the concepts that are being used.

If religious concepts and formulae are merely repeated without any such effort being made, their level of meaningfulness will decline. There is a phenomenon known as 'semantic satiation',[44] which has been demonstrated in psychological research, that provides an analogue of this phenomenon. If people repeat a word over and over, or if they stare fixedly at it for a few minutes, attention shifts to the word's visual features or to the sound made in pronouncing it, and it loses subjective meaningfulness. Though the use of words in liturgy is not as intensive as in these artificial experiments, it is possible that a similar phenomenon of semantic satiation can take place through too frequent repetition. Too much repetition of invariant language can be the anvil on which meaningfulness is broken.

However, semantic satiation is not an inevitable consequence of the over frequent use of words. If people do something that reminds them of the meaning of the word, semantic satiation is less likely to take place. A laboratory example of this is that if people do appropriate actions while repeating words like 'push' or 'lift' these words do not lose their subjective meaningfulness as quickly.[45] A number of tasks have been found that successfully direct attention to the meaning of the words such as rating words for pleasantness, writing down associated words, thinking of associated visual images. Such tasks dramatically improve memory for the words to which they have been applied.[46] In contrast, if people focus their attention on superficial aspects of words such as what they look or sound like, their memory for them is relatively poor. The fairly common phenomenon of reading a page of print, and realising at the end that one has no idea of the content, is an everyday example of attending to the look or sound of words, but grasping their meaning only to a very limited extent.

The use of religious language in prayer and liturgy can sometimes be accompanied by relatively little attention to the meanings of the word. In contrast, there are meditative exercises that seem designed explicitly to counteract this. The advice of Ignatius Loyola about the use of words of the Lord's Prayer is typical.[47] The person using this method 'says Father, and rests on the consideration of this word for so long a time as he finds meanings, comparisons, relish and consolation in considerations belonging to such a word'. In this way, he thinks 'quietly and simply of each word, drawing out the meaning of it'. Other methods of meditation make similar use of mental pictures or exercises involving imagery from the various senses to set something of importance before the person who prays, experience it as vividly as possible, grasp its significance and respond to it. In each case,

few words or images are used. There is no hurry to pass on from one
to the next. Time is spent grasping the meaning of the words or images
used at the deepest level possible.

Such an approach to the use of religious concepts is appropriate
to their 'emblematic' character. Double-aspect concepts of God,
which are the simplest religious concepts, show clearly the coalescence
of meanings that is characteristic of religious thinking, and which is
found in even more complex forms in mythical, sacramental and
doctrinal concepts. Maintaining the resonance of such religious
concepts is a painstaking, creative act.

# 10

# Recapitulation

## *Is religious knowing possible?*

If, to some people, religious knowing seems an impossibility, that is perhaps because they have not grasped what the expression might mean. The concept of religious knowing does not necessarily entail that there is a separate religious world that we can know in exactly the same way as we know the external world of nature and man-made objects. It is this erroneous concept of religious knowing that has led many people to think, either that blind faith is all that is possible in religion, or that religion is mere superstitious nonsense.

There are many kinds of knowing, with family resemblances, but each with distinct features. The relative neglect of this consideration has limited the ability of cognitive psychology to give an account of religious knowing, as indeed of aesthetic cognition, personal insight and much more. These neglected forms of knowing arise in a space that transcends a crude dichotomy into what is objective and what is subjective.

In understanding the nature of such forms of knowing, style is perhaps more important than content. They require patience, commitment and careful attention to experience, but they also require intellectual and emotional restraint. They depend upon being able to bring apparently disparate ideas together in consciousness so that connections can be experienced and articulated.

Religious knowing involves, not so much coming to know a separate religious world, as coming to know the religious dimension of the everyday world. To acknowledge this is to be faithful, both to how religious knowing proceeds in practice, and to the traditional religious understanding that the everyday world is one that God created, in which he has incarnated, and in which he can be discerned by those ready to do so.

It is with an interactional reality, not with a separate religious reality, that religious knowing is concerned. Taking the step to a religious perception of the world is like moving from a narrow form of medicine that sees the body as a self-contained mechanism to a psychosomatic medicine that sees it as interacting with psychological processes. Religious knowing is concerned with a world in which the spiritual and the material interact; both everyday concepts and religious concepts are enriched by this interactionalist perspective. For religious people, discerning the hand of God in events enriches both the meaningfulness of their lives and their understanding of God.

## *Religious and personal insight*

Religious knowing is a highly personal process that is both similar to, and intertwined with, knowledge of ourselves. Religious and personal insights arise as a result of similar cognitive processes and have many common features. The religious person approaches both with the same seriousness of purpose, for in aspiring to a truer knowledge of himself, and in basing his life upon this, he discerns the nature and purposes of God more clearly. Religious insights, like personal insights can burst upon us suddenly, though often after a period of gestation. More commonly they are hard-won after long effort and struggle. Indeed we should be suspicious of adopting either personal or religious insights too easily, because we may be doing nothing more than striking a superficial attitude about ourselves that sits uneasily with the truth. The validity of both personal and religious insights is difficult to assess, but there is nothing to be gained from searching for either unless we have the integrity to evaluate them honestly and conscientiously.

The quest for both personal and religious insight requires openness. We need to look beyond what is obvious and what it is convenient to acknowledge. To gain personal insight we may need to set aside stereotyped ruminations about ourselves; to gain religious insight we may need to set aside doctrinal clichés or religious obsessions. Once the necessary space has been created, we need to learn attentiveness that is broad, sustained and penetrating. Finally, there is the struggle to conceptualise our insights. At first this will probably be halting and based around a few seminal ideas, later it may become more fluent and systematic.

## The middle way

With religious knowing, it is always necessary to find a middle way:

- it requires seriousness of purpose, but lightness of touch;
- it cannot thrive either when peoples' emotions are uninvolved or when they are unrestrained;
- it requires a sense of relatedness to God that is neither one of identification with Him nor of alienation from Him;
- it is a matter neither of pure faith nor of pure reason;
- it is not independent of observation, but neither does it follow straightforwardly from it;
- it inhabits the realms, neither of private fantasy nor of external reality, but a space between;
- it is a creative act, that goes beyond the 'given' but must be faithful to it;
- it shows a capacity, in myth and sacrament, to make connections that are more than merely symbolic representations of literal truths, but without going so far as to confound the symbol with the symbolised;
- it depends on the combination of both genuine personal experience and the effort to articulate it, for neither alone can lead to knowing;
- it requires the intellectual effort and clear-headedness to reach towards religious knowing wherever possible, but also the recognition that there is a time for silence and not-knowing.

# Notes

## 2. Psychological research on religion

1. G. E. W. Scobie, *Psychology of Religion* (London, Batsford, 1975); B. Spilka, R. W. Hood, and R. L. Gorsuch, *The Psychology of Religion: An Empirical Approach* (Englewood Cliffs, N. J., Prentice-Hall, 1985).
2. C. Y. Glock, 'On the study of religious commitment', *Religious Research Supplement*, 57 (1962), 98–110.
3. M. B. King and R. A. Hunt, 'Measuring the religious variable: reflections', *Journal for the Scientific Study of Religion*, 11, (1972), 240–51.
4. Independent Television Authority, *Religion in Britain and Northern Ireland* (London, ITA, 1970).
5. M. Argyle and B. Beit-Hallahmi, *The Social Psychology of Religion* (London, Routledge and Kegan Paul, 1975).
6. M. Argyle and B. Beit-Hallahmi, *op. cit.*
7. R. O. Allen and B. Spilka 'Committed and consensual religion: a specification of religion-prejudice relationships', *Journal for the Scientific Study of Religion*, 6 (1967), 191–206.
8. M. Argyle, *Religious Behaviour*, (Glencoe, Free Press, 1959).
9. G. W. Allport, 'The religious context of prejudice', *Journal for the Scientific Study of Religion*, 5 (1966), 447–57.
10. R. D. Allen and B. Spilka, *op. cit.*
11. G. W. Allport and J. M. Ross 'Personal religious orientation and prejudice', *Journal of Personality and Social Psychology*, 5 (1967), 432–43.
12. J. Piaget, *Child's Construction of Reality* (London, Routledge and Kegan Paul, 1955).
13. See B. Spilka et al, *op. cit.*, chapter 3; D. Elkind, 'The origins of religion in the child', *Review of Religious Research*, 12 (1970), 35–42. A particularly interesting application of a Piagetian stage development theory to religious development in adulthood is J. W. Fowler, *Stages of Faith* (New York, Harper and Row, 1981).
14. R. Goldman, *Religious Thinking from Childhood to Adolescence* (London, Routledge and Kegan Paul, 1964).
15. R. Goldman, *Readiness for Religion* (London, Routledge and Kegan Paul, 1969).
16. W. James, *Varieties of Religious Experience* (New York, Longmans, 1902), p. 337.
17. B. Spilka et al, *op. cit.*, chapter 7.
18. W. T. Stace, *Mysticism and Philosophy* (New York, Macmillan, 1960).
19. R. W. Hood, 'The construction and preliminary validation of a measure of reported mystical experience', *Journal for the Scientific Study of Religion*, 14 (1975), 29–41.
20. R. Hood, 'Mystical experience as related to present and anticipated future church participation', *Psychological Reports*, 39 (1976), 1127–36.
21. D. Hay, *Exploring Inner Space: Scientists and Religious Experience* (Harmondsworth, Penguin, 1982).

22. A.M. Greeley, *Ecstasy: A Way of Knowing* (Englewood Cliffs, N. J., Prentice-Hall, 1974).
23. D. Hay, *op. cit.*, pp. 133–4.
24. See B. Spilka et al, *op. cit.*, chapter 7.
25. D. Hay, *op. cit.*, p. 137.
26. D. Hay, *op. cit.*, p. 138.
27. D. Hay, *op. cit.*, p. 159.

## 3. Psychoanalytic approaches to religious experience

1. S. Freud, *Totem and Taboo*, Standard Edition of the complete psychological words, vol. 13 (London, Hogarth, 1951).
2. S. Freud, *The Future of an Illusion*, Standard Edition, vol. 21 (London, Hogarth, 1951).
3. S. Freud, *Moses and Monotheism*, Standard Edition, vol. 23 (London, Hogarth, 1951).
4. P. Ricœur, *Freud and Philosophy: An Essay on Interpretation* (New Haven, Yale University Press, 1970).
5. W. W. Meissner, *Psychoanalysis and Religious Experience* (New Haven, Yale University Press, 1984).
6. B. Spilka et al, *op. cit.*
7. H. Meng and E. L. Freud (eds), *Psychoanalysis and Faith: The Letters of Sigmund Freud and Oskar Pfister* (New York, Basic Books, 1963).
8. C. G. Jung, Psychology of the Unconscious, In H. Read, M. Fordham, G. Adler (eds) *The Collected Works of C. G. Jung*, vol. 7 (London, Routledge and Kegan Paul, 1953).
9. C. G. Jung, 'Answer to Job', In H. Read, M. Fordham and G. Adler (eds) *The Collected Works of C. G. Jung*, vol. 11 (London, Routledge and Kegan Paul, 1958).
10. C. G. Jung, *Psychology and Alchemy*, in H. Read, M Fordham and G. Adler (eds) *Collected Works of C. G. Jung*, vol. 12 (London, Routledge and Kegan Paul, 1953).
11. J . W. Heisig, *Imago Dei: A Study in C. G. Jung's Psychology of Religion* (London, Associated University Presses).
12. S. Freud, *A Seventeenth Century Demonological Neurosis*, Standard Edition, vol. 19 (London, Hogarth, 1951). For a good exposition of Freud's views see A.-M. Rizzuto, *The Birth of the Living God: A Psychoanalytic Study* (Chicago, University of Chicago Press, 1979).
13. For a good exposition and critical review of the concept of archetype see chapter 2 in A. Samuels, *Jung and the Post-Jungians* (London, Routledge and Kegan Paul, 1985).
14. R. Otto, *The Idea of the Holy: An Inquiry into the non-rational factor in the idea of the divine and its relation to the rational* (2nd ed., Trans. J. W. Harvey, Oxford, Oxford University Press, 1950).
15. James Hillman, *Revisioning Psychology* (New York, Harper and Row, 1975).
16. E. Fromm, *Psychoanalysis and Religion* (New Haven, Yale University Press, 1950).
17. H. Meng and E. L. Freud (eds) *Psychoanalysis and Faith: The Letters of Sigmund Freud and Oskar Pfister* (New York, Basic Books, 1963).
18. O. Pfister, 'Die Illusion einer Zukunft' (The illusion of a future) *Imago*, 14 (1928), 149–84, p. 158.
19. A. Godin, *The Psychological Dynamics of Religious Experience* (Birmingham, Alabama, Religious Education Press, 1985).

20. D. W. Winnicott, *Playing and Reality* (New York, Basic Books, 1971). See also S. A. Grolnick and L. Barkin (eds), *Between Fantasy and Reality: The Transitional Object* (New York, Aronson, 1978).
21. P. W. Pruyser, *Between Belief and Unbelief* (Sheldon Press, London, 1974). P. W. Pruyser, *The Play of Imagination. Towards a Psychoanalysis of Culture* (New York, International Universities Press, 1983).
22. A.-M. Rizzuto, *op. cit.*
23. W. W. Meissner, *op. cit.*
24. S. Freud, *The Future of an Illusion, op. cit.*, p. 31.
25. P. Pruyser, *Between Belief and Unbelief, op. cit.*, p. 111.
26. D. W. Winnicott, *Playing and Reality, op. cit.*, p. 2.
27. W. W. Meissner, *op. cit.*, p. 183—4.
28. See O. Barfield, *What Coleridge Thought* (Middletown, Wesleyan University Press, 1971).
29. M. Burber, *Between Man and Man*, trans R. G. Smith (London, Collins, 1961), see especially 'What is Man?'
30. A. M. Rizzutto, *op. cit.*

## 4. Faith and knowledge

1. Of the voluminous literature available, the following may be of particular interest: B. Blanshard, *Reason and Belief* (London, George Allen and Unwin, 1974); W. C. Smith, *Faith and Belief* (Princeton, N. J., Princeton University Press, 1979), R. Swinburn, *Faith and Reason* (Oxford, Clarendon Press, 1981); F. J. Crosson (ed), *The Autonomy of Religious Belief* (Notre Dame, University of Notre Dame Press, 1981); A. Plantings and N. Woltersorff (eds.) *Faith and Rationality* (Notre Dame, University of Notre Dame Press, 1983).
2. J. Hick, *Faith and Knowledge*, 2nd edition (London, Macmillan, 1967). (In some of his later writings, Hick has become less of a cognitivist than he was in *Faith and Knowledge*.)
3. J. Kellenberger, *Religious Discovery, Faith and Knowledge* (Englewood Cliffs, Prentice Hall, 1972); J. Kellenberger, *The Cognitivity of Religion: Three Perspectives* (London, Macmillan, 1985).
4. See especially V. White, *Holy Teaching* (Oxford, Blackwell, 1958); V. Preller, *Divine Science and the Science of God* (New Jersey, Princeton University Press, 1967).
5. A. Kenny, *The Five Ways: St Thomas Aquinas' Proofs of God's Existence* (London, Routledge and Kegan Paul, 1969).
6. See D. Burrell, *Aquinas: God and Action* (London, Routledge and Kegan Paul, 1979).
7. An interesting early example of the rational case for the existence of God, first published in 1802, is W. Paley, *Natural Theology* (Godstone, Gregg Internation, 1970).
8. A. J. Ayer, *Language, Truth and Logic* (London, Gollancz, 1936).
9. A. Flew, 'Theology and falsification', In A. Flew and A. MacIntyre (eds) *New Essays in Philosophical Theology* (London, SCM Press, 1955).
10. R. Braithwaite, *An Empiricist's View of the Nature of Religious Belief* (Cambridge, Cambridge University Press, 1955).
11. T. McPherson, 'Religion as the inexpressible'. In A. Flew and A. MacIntyre (eds) *op. cit.*

12. P. M. Van Buren, *The Secular Meaning of the Gospel based on an Analysis of its Language* (London, SCM Press, 1963).

13. See T. Penelhum, *God and Scepticism: A Study in Scepticism and Fideism* (Dordrecht, Reidel, 1983).

14. For a convenient exposition see G. V. Bromiley, *An Introduction to the Theology of Karl Barth* (Edinburgh, T. and T. Clark, 1979), chapter 5.

15. A good exposition and appraisal can be found in K. Nielsen, *An Introduction to the Philosophy of Religion* (London, Macmillan, 1982).

16. L. Wittgenstein, *Culture and Value* (Oxford, Blackwell, 1980), p. 53.

17. L. Wittgenstein, 'A Lecture on Ethics', *Philosophical Review*, 74 (1965), 3—12.

18. L. Wittgenstein, *Lectures and Conversations on Aesthetics, Psychology, and Religious Belief* (Oxford, Blackwell, 1966).

19. D. Z. Phillips, *The Concept of Prayer* (Oxford, Basil Blackwell, 1965).

20. N. Malcolm, 'Is it a religious belief that "God exists"?' In J. Hick (ed.) *Faith and the Philosophers* (London, Macmillan, 1964). See K. Neilson, *op. cit.*, for a discussion of Malcolm's paper.

21. A. J. Plantinga, *God and Other Minds* (Oxford, Oxford University Press, 1968).

22. A. J. Ayer, *The Foundations of Empirical Knowledge* (London, Macmillan, 1940), p. 45.

23. L. Wittgenstein, *On Certainty* (Oxford, Blackwell, 1975).

24. C. B. Martin, 'A religious way of knowing' in A. Flew and A. Macintyre (eds.), *op. cit.*.

25. There has been surprising neglect of the distinctive contribution of, and scope for integration between, the philosophical and psychological approaches to knowledge and knowing. An early attempt that influenced our thinking was J. R. Royce and W. W. Rozeboom (eds.), *The Psychology of Knowing* (New York, Gordon and Breach, 1972). A major recent contribution is A. I. Goldman, *Epistemology and Cognition* (Harvard, Harvard University Press, 1986).

26. I. G. Barbour, *Myths, Models and Paradigms: The Nature of Scientific and Religious Language* (London, SCM Press, 1974).

27. N. R. Hanson, *Patterns of Discovery* (Cambridge, Cambridge University Press, 1958).

28. T. S. Kuhn, *The Structure of Scientific Revolutions*, 2nd ed. (Chicago, Chicago University Press, 1970).

29. B. G. Mitchell, *The Justification of Religious Belief* (London, Macmillan, 1973).

30. See, for example, I. T. Ramsey, *Models and Mystery* (Oxford, Oxford University Press, 1964).

31. J. Kellenberger, *Religious Discovery, Faith and Knowledge, op. cit.*

32. R. L. Gregory, *Eye and Brain* (London, Weidenfeld and Nicolson, 1966).

33. J. Kellenberger, *The Cognitivity of Religion: Three Perspectives* (London, Macmillan, 1985).

34. St Bonaventura, *The Mind's Road to God*, trans. G. Boas (New York, Bobbs-Merrill, 1953), p. 13.

35. M. Polany, *Personal Knowledge: Towards a Post-critical Philosophy* (London, Routledge and Kegan Paul, 1958).

36. See R. Avens, *The New Gnosis: Heidegger, Hillman and Angels* (Dallas, Spring Publications, 1984).

37. G. L. Phillips, 'Faith and vision in the fourth gospel' in F. L. Cross (ed.), *Studies in the Fourth Gospel* (London, A. R. Mowbray, 1957). Though Phillips case is well argued, other scholars have been more inclined to the view that the various words for 'see' are interchanged randomly.

38. See R. Williams, *The Wound of Knowledge: Christian Spirituality from the New Testament to St John of the Cross* (London, Darton, Longman and Todd, 1979), pp. 122–30.

39. Cited in R. Avens, *op. cit.*, p. 3.

40. C. G. Jung, *The Undiscovered Self* (London, Routledge and Kegan Paul, 1958), p. 74.

41. Outside the circle of his followers there has been an unfortunate tendency to ignore Rudolf Steiner (1861–1925), the Austrian polymath and spiritual leader, presumably because of doubts about the reliability of his method of 'spiritual science' and puzzlement about the gulf between ordinary experience and a good deal of what he taught. Nevertheless, we have found much of value in his work. He attempted to relate to radically spiritual world view to the twentieth-century philosophical and scientific climate on a broader front, and with greater conceptual coherence, than can be found almost anywhere else. A recent popular discussion of the 'puzzle' presented by Steiner is C. Wilson, *Rudolf Steiner: The Man and His Vision* (Wellingborough, Aquarian Press, 1985). For an introduction to his psychology, see F. N. Watts, 'The Spiritual Psychology of Rudolf Steiner'. In G. Glaxton (Ed.), *Beyond Therapy* (London, Wisdom Publications, 1986). For his views on faith and knowledge, see R. Steiner, *The Redemption of Thinking: A Study in the Philosophy of Thomas Aquinas*, trans. A. P. Shepherd and M. R. Nicoll, (London, Hodder and Stoughton, 1956).

42. C. Davy, *Towards a Third Culture* (London, Faber and Faber, 1961).

## 5. Analogues of religious cognition

1. M. S. Lindauer, 'Aesthetic experience: a neglected topic in the psychology of the arts'. In D. O'Hare (ed), *Psychology and The Arts* (Sussex, Harvester Press, 1981).

2. H. Osborne, *The Art of Appreciation* (London, Oxford University Press, 1970).

3. J. Bruner, 'Art as a mode of knowing'. In J. Bruner, *On Knowing: Essays for the Left Hand*, expanded edition (Cambridge, Mass., Harvard University Press, 1979).

4. E. Bullough, *Aesthetics: Lectures and Essays* (London, Bowes and Bowes, 1957).

5. J. Bruner, 'Art as a mode of knowing', *op. cit.*, pp. 70–2.

6. E. Bullough, *op. cit.*, p. 174.

7. S. Weil, 'Reflection on the right use of school studies with a view to the love of God'. In S. Weil, *Waiting on God* (London, Routledge and Kegan Paul, 1951).

8. R. L. Katz, *Empathy: Its Nature and Uses* (New York, Free Press, 1963).

9. See H. C. Smith, *Sensitivity to People* (New York, MacGraw Hill, 1966); F. N. Watts, 'Clinical Judgement and Clinical Training', *British Journal of Medical Psychology*, 53 (1980), 95–108.

10. T. Reik, *Listening with the Third Ear* (New York, Farrar Strauss, 1948).

11. P. Casement, *On Learning from the Patient* (London, Tavistock, 1985).

12. A. J. Deikman, 'Experimental Meditation', *Journal of Nervous and Mental Diseases*, 136 (1963); 'Deautomatisation and the msytic experience', *Psychiatry*, 29 (1966), 324–38; 'Bimodel consciousness', *Archives of General Psychiatry*, 25 (1971), 481–9.

13. D. P. Brown, 'A model for the levels of concentration meditation', *International Journal of Clinical and Experimental Hypnosis*, 24 (1977), 236–73.

14. T. Halwes, 'Structural realism, coalitions, and the relationship of Gibsonian, constructivist and Buddhist theories of preception' in W. B. Weimer and D. S. Palermo (eds) *Cognition and the Symbolic Processes* (New York, Lawrence Erlbaum, 1974).

15. D.P. Brown, *op. cit.*
16. H.A. Wilkin, R.B. Dyk, H.F. Faterson, D.R. Goodenough and S.A. Karp, *Psychological Differentiation* (New York, John Wiley, 1962).
17. See, for example, W. Linden 'Practising of meditation by schoolchildren at their levels of field-dependence/independence, test anxiety and reading achievement,' *Journal of Consulting and Clinical Psychology*, 41 (1973), 139–43.
18. There is a clear and convenient account of Goethe's method, originally described in his *Metamorphosis of Plants*, in E. Lehrs, *Mass or Matter*, 2nd ed. (London, Faber and Faber, 1958), part 2.
19. H.A. Wilkin et al., *op. cit.*
20. T.V. Lesh, 'Zen meditation and the development of empathy in counsellors', *Journal of Humanistic Psychology*, 10 (1970), 39–74.
21. A readable account of Kohlberg's position and a discussion of its religious implications can be found in R. Duska and M. Whelan, *Moral Development* (Dublin, Gill and MacMillan, 1977).
22. A.J. Newman, 'Aesthetic sensitizing and moral education', *Journal of Aesthetic Education*, 14 (1980), 93–101.
23. M. Ross, 'Knowing face to face: towards mature aesthetic encountering'. In M. Ross (ed) *The Development of Aesthetic Experience* (Oxford, Pergamon, 1982).
24. I. Murdoch, *The Sovereignty of Good* (London, Routledge and Kegan Paul, 1970).
25. See for example R. Wollheim, *The Thread of Life* (Cambridge, Cambridge University Press, 1985).
26. See chapter 10 in J. Sandler, C. Dare and A. Holder, *The Patient and the Analyst: The Basis of the Psychoanalytic Process* (London, George Allen and Unwin, 1973).
27. J.H. Newman, *An Essay in Aid of a Grammar of Assent* (Oxford, Oxford University Press, 1985). There is a discussion of Newman's position in J. Hick, *Faith and Knowledge*, 2nd ed. (London, Macmillan, 1967).
28. E.T. Gendlin, *Experiencing and the Creation of Meaning* (Glencoe, Free Press, 1962).
29. A discussion of this parallel and other aspects of religious knowing can be found in chapter 5 of J. Havens (ed), *Psychology and Religion* (Princeton, N.J., Van Nostrand, 1968).
30. S.T. Katz (ed), *Mysticism and Religious Traditions* (Oxford, Oxford University Press, 1983).
31. *Meister Eckhart*, trans. R.B. Blakney (New York, Harper and Row, 1941).
32. V. Lossky, *The Mystical Theology of the Eastern Church* (Cambridge, James Clark, 1957).
33. *The Cloud of Unknowing*, ed. J. Walsh (London, SPCK, 1982). The author is thought to have been a country clergyman of the late fourteenth century.

## 6. Emotional regulation and religious attentiveness

1. See chapter 7 in R.H. Thouless, *An Introduction to the Psychology of Religion*, 3rd ed. (Cambridge, Cambridge University Press, 1971).
2. J.W. Povah, *The New Psychology and the Hebrew Prophets* (New York, Longman, 1925).
3. J. Jaynes, *The Origin of Consciousness in the Breakdown of the Bicameral Mind* (London, Allen Lane, 1979).

4. R. L. Woolfolk, 'Psychophysiological correlates of meditation', *Archives of General Psychiatry*, 32 (1975), 1326–33. The one rigorous and thorough empirical study of Christian contemplation to have been reported is M. M. Mallory, *Christian Mysticism: Transcending Techniques* (Assen, Van Gorcum, 1977).

5. D. H. Shapiro, *Meditation: Self-Regulation Strategy and Altered States of Consciousness* (New York, Aldine, 1980).

6. D. S. Holmes, 'Meditation and somatic arousal reduction: a review of the evidence,' *American Psychologist*, 39 (1984), 1–10.

7. M. J. Horowitz, *Image Formation and Psychotherapy* (New York, Jason Aronson, 1983).

8. J. L. Singer, *Daydreaming and Fantasy* (Oxford, Oxford University Press, 1981).

9. M. W. Eysenck, *Attention and Arousal* (Berlin, Springer-Verlag, 1982).

10. A. Baker, *Holy Wisdom*, Wheathampstead, Anthony Clarke Books, 1964, p. 70.

11. R. Steiner, *Occult Science*, trans. F. and M. Adams (London, Rudolf Steiner Press, 1962), p. 245.

12. H. Suso, *The Life of the Servant*, trans. J. M. Clark (London, J. Clark, 1952).

13. *The Letters of William Blake*, 2nd edition (London, Rupert Hart-Davis, 1968), p. 154.

14. Only a proportion of the claims of Freudian psychology have been subjected to verification by conventional scientific methods, and reviewers differ in their judgements about how favourable the results have been. A sample of the primary scientific material can be found in S. Fisher and R. P. Greenberg (eds) *The Scientific Evaluation of Freud's Theories and Therapy* (Hassocks, Harvester, 1978). See also B. A. Farrell, *The Standing of Psychoanalysis* (Oxford, Oxford University Press, 1981) and P. Kline, *Fact and Fantasy in Freudian Theory* (London, Methuen, 1981).

15. R. C. Bolles, *Learning Theory*, 2nd edition (London, Holt, Rinehart and Winston, 1979).

16. M. M. Mallory, *Christian Mysticism: Transcending Techniques* (Assen, van Gorcum, 1977).

17. A. Baker, *op. cit.*, p. 204.

18. R. Steiner, *op. cit.*, pp. 247–8.

19. R. Hinde, 'Energy models of motivation,' *Symposium of the Society of Experimental Biology*, 14 (1960), 199–210.

20. See S. P. Grossman, *A Textbook of Physiological Psychology* (New York, John Wiley, 1967). Homeostatic drives are reduced by consummatory activities; this does not occur in non-homeostatic drives.

21. L. Berkowitz, *Aggression: A Social Psychological Analysis* (New York, McGraw-Hill, 1962).

22. A. Baker, *op. cit.*, p. 179.

23. A. Baker, *op. cit.*, p. 236.

24. P. de Silva, 'Buddhism and Behaviour Modification', *Behaviour Research and Therapy*, 22 (1984), 661–78.

25. R. Steiner, *op. cit.*, pp. 247–8.

26. See J. Sandler, C. Dare and A. Holder, *The Patient and the Analyst* (London, George Allen and Unwin, 1973).

27. P. Carrington and H. S. Ephron 'Meditation as an adjunct to psychotherapy' in S. Arieti (ed) *New Dimensions in Psychiatry: A World View* (New York, Wiley, 1975).

28. M. West, 'Meditation', *British Journal of Psychiatry*, 135 (1979), 457–67.

29. A. Ellis, *Reason and Emotion in Psychotherapy* (New York, Lyle Stuart, 1962).

30. Quoted by P. de Silva, *op cit.*, p. 670.

31. J. M. G. Williams, *The Psychological Treatment of Depression* (London, Croom Helm, 1984).

## 7. Self knowledge and knowledge of God

1. There is a discussion of some related issues in W. Proudfoot, *God and the Self* (Lewisburg, Bucknell University Press, 1976). However, the approach here is more from the standpoint of epistemology than from cognitive psychology.
2. J. Jaynes, *The Origins of Consciousness in the Breakdown of the Bicameral Mind* (London, Allen Lane, 1976); J. H. Crook, *The Evolution of Human Consciousness* (Oxford, Oxford University Press, 1980). E. Neumann, *The Origins and History of Conciousness*, (Princeton, N.J., Princeton University Press, 1954). An important recent study of post-mediaeval changes in the sense of self is R. F. Baumeister, *Identity* (Oxford, Oxford University Press, 1986).
3. W. E. Houghton, *The Victorian Frame of Mind, 1830—1870* (London, Yale University Press, 1957).
4. See I. Murdoch, *Sartre: Romantic Rationalist* (Cambridge, Bowes and Bowes, 1953).
5. L. Trilling, *Sincerity and Authenticity* (London, Oxford University Press, 1974), pp. 12—13.
6. A. MacIntyre, *A Short History of Ethics* (London, Routledge and Kegan Paul, 1967).
7. See, for example, R. Harre, *Social Being* (Oxford, Blackwell, 1979).
8. O. Barfield, *History in English Words* (London, Faber and Faber, 1953). A related point, drawing on the literature of the eighteenth century is made in a book whose title vividly captures its theme: J. O. Lyons, *The Invention of the Self: The Hinge of Consciousness in the Late Eighteenth Century* (London, Feffer and Simmons, 1978).
9. J. Hillman, *Revisioning Psychology* (New York, Harper and Row, 1975), pp. 193—7.
10. O. Barfield, *Saving the Appearances: A Study in Idolatry* (London, Faber and Faber, 1957).
11. H. Werner, *Comparative Psychology of Mental Development* (Chicago, Follett Publishing Company, 1948). See also E. G. Schachtel, *Metamorphosis* (New York, Basic Books, 1959). The concept of primitive mentality has had a sceptical reception within anthropology, as for example in J. W. Rogerson, *Anthropology and the Old Testament* (Oxford, Basil Blackwell, 1978). The problem seems to be that increasing evidence for the sophistication of earlier societies has made people reluctant to use disparaging terms such as 'primitive'. However, it cannot readily be denied that there are at least qualitative differences in the thought-patterns of earlier societies from our own.
12. J. Barr, *The Semantics of Biblical Language* (Oxford, Oxford University Press, 1961). See also F. Hiebel, *The Epistles of Paul and Rudolf Steiner's Philosophy of Freedom* (New York, St George Publications, 1980). Hiebel is much influenced by the work on the concept of conscience of the classical philologist, Friedrich Zucker.
13. See also, O. Barfield, *Saving the Appearances, op. cit.*, pp. 156—86; O. Barfield, *The Rediscovery of Meaning and Other Essays* (Middletown, Wesleyan University Press, 1977), pp. 228—60.
14. See K. Nordentoft, *Kierkegaard's Psychology* (Pittsburgh, Duquesne University Press, 1978).
15. D. Cairns, *The Image of God in Man* (London, SCM Press, 1953).
16. P. Tillich, *Theology of Culture* (Oxford, Oxford University Press, 1959), pp. 10—11.

17. For good expositions of Jung's concepts of the ego and the Self, see A. Samuels, *Jung and the Post-Jungians* (London, Routledge and Kegan Paul, 1985); and J. W. T. Redfearn, *My Self: My Many Selves* (London, Academic Press, 1986).

18. In Jung's early work, the term 'godlikeness' was used consistently, but, from around 1917, it was replaced by the more technical term 'inflation'. See D. L. Miller, 'Red Riding Hood and Grand Mother Rhea', in J. Hillman et al, *Facing the Gods* (Dallas, Spring Publications, 1980). For a discussion of religious inflation in the Freudian tradition, see T. Reik, 'From spell to prayer,' *Psychoanalysis*, 3 (1955), 3–26.

19. J. Hillman, *Insearch: Psychology and Religion* (New York, Hodder and Stoughton, 1967), p. 23. For a classical account of the teaching of St Bernard, see E. Gilson, *The Mystical Theology of St Bernard* (London, Sheed and Ward, 1940).

20. W. Mischel, *Personality and Assessment* (New York, John Wiley, 1968).

21. S. Kierkegaard, *The Sickness unto Death* (Princeton, N.J., Princeton University Press, 1968), p. 153.

22. S. Kierkegaard, *Concluding Unscientific Postscipt* (Princeton, N.J., Princeton University Press, 1941), p. 218.

23. S. Kierkegaard, *The Sickness unto Death, op. cit.*, p. 163.

24. R. Harré and P. F. Secord, *The Explanation of Social Behaviour* (Oxford, Blackwell, 1972).

25. D. Emmet, *Function, Purpose and Powers* (London, Macmillan, 1958).

26. See M. Sherwood, *The Logic of Explanation in Psychoanalysis* (New York, Academic Press, 1969), pp. 244–257; B. A. Farrell, *The Standing of Psychoanalysis* (Oxford, Oxford University Press, 1981), chapter 5.

27. W. James, *Textbook of Psychology: Briefer Course* (New York, Holt, 1890). On concepts of the self, see also P. A. Bertocci, 'The psychological self, the ego and personality', *Psychological Review*, 52 (1945), 91–9.

28. D. J. Bem, 'Self perception theory', *Advances in Experimental Social Psychology*, 6 (1972), 1–62.

29. P. D. Ashworth, *Social Interaction and Consciousness* (Chichester, John Wiley, 1979).

30. C. T. Tart (ed), *Transpersonal Psychologies* (London, Routledge and Kegan Paul, 1975).

31. For a psychological commentary from a Jungian standpoint, see J. Welch, *Spiritual Pilgrims: Carl Jung and Teresa of Avila* (New York, Paulist Press, 1982).

32. P. Kelvin, *The Bases of Social Behavior* (London, Holt, Rinehart and Winston, 1969).

33. See F. N. Watts and D. H. Bennett (eds), *Theory and Practice of Psychiatric Rehabilitation* (Chichester, John Wiley, 1983), chapter 14.

34. K. Danziger, *Socialization* (Harmondsworth, Penguin, 1971).

35. See A. Samuels, *Jung and the Post-Jungians* (London, Routledge and Kegan Paul, 1985), chapter 4.

36. S. Kierkegaard, *The Sickness unto Death, op. cit.*, p. 163.

37. S. Kierkegaard, *Christian Discourses* (Oxford, Oxford University Press, 1940) pp. 340–1.

38. I. Berlin, *Two Concepts of Liberty* (Oxford, Clarendon Press, 1958).

39. S. Brehm and J. Brehm, *Psychological Reactance* (London, Academic Press, 1981).

40. G. A. Kelly, *The Psychology of Personal Constructs* (New York, Norton, 1955).

41. R. Steiner, *The Philosophy of Freedom*, trans. M. Wilson (London, Rudolf Steiner Press, 1964).

## 8. The interpretation of experience in prayer

1. R. Goldman, *Religious Thinking from Childhood to Adolescence* (London, Routledge and Kegan Paul, 1964), chapter 12.
2. D. Long, D. Elkind and B. Spilka, 'The child's conception of prayer,' *Journal for the Scientific Study of Religion*, 6 (1967), 101–9.
3. Cited in F. Heiler, *Prayer: A Study in the History and Psychology of Religion*, trans. S. McComb (New York, Oxford University Press, 1958), p. 234. Chapter 9 contains a good analysis of urgent personal prayer, and abundant examples.
4. D. Hay, *Exploring Inner Space* (Harmondsworth, Penguin, 1982).
5. J. Macquarrie, *The Faith of the People of God* (London, SCM, 1972), p. 95.
6. D. Z. Phillips, *The Concept of Prayer* (Oxford, Blackwell, 1965).
7. W. James, *Varieties of Religious Experience* (New York, Longmans, 1902).
8. S. Kierkegaard, *Purity of Heart*, trans. D. Steeve (London, Fontana, 1961), p. 44.
9. S. Kierkegaard, *op. cit.*, pp. 44–5.
10. J. Macquarrie, *op. cit.*, p. 99.
11. See, for example, G. W. Brown and T. Harris, *Social Origins of Depression* (London, Tavistock, 1978); R. Totman, *Social Causes of Illness* (London, Souvenir Press, 1979).
12. C. M. Parkes, *Bereavement*, (Harmondsworth, Penguin, 1975).
13. V. Frankl, *Psychotherapy and Existentialism* (Harmondsworth, Penguin, 1973).
14. J. H. Harvey and C. Weary, *Perspectives on Attributional Processes* (Iowa, Wm. C. Brown and Co., 1981).
15. See J. M. G. Williams, *The Psychological Treatment of Depression* (London, Croom Helm, 1984).
16. See B. Spilka, R. W. Hood and R. L. Gorsuch, *The Psychology of Religion: An Empirical Approach* (Englewood Cliffs, Prentice-Hall, 1985), pp. 17–28.
17. W. W. Meissner, *Psychoanalysis and Religious Experience* (New Haven, Yale University Press, 1984), p. 182.
18. J. O. Raynor 'Future orientation and motivation of immediate activity', *Psychological Review* 76 (1969), 606–10.
19. D. Z. Phillips, *op. cit.*, pp. 101–6.
20. J. Hillman, *Revisioning Psychology* (New York, Harper and Row, 1975).
21. H. J. Einhorn and R. M. Hogarth, 'Confidence in judgement, persistence of the illusion of validity', *Psychological Review*, 85 (1978), 395–416.
22. A. Ulanov and B. Ulanov, *Primary Speech: A Psychology of Prayer* (London, SCM Press, 1985), especially chapter 6.
23. P. Casement, *On Learning from the Patient* (London, Tavistock, 1985).
24. S. J. Blatt, D. M. Quinlan, E. S. Chevron, C. McDonald and D. Zuroff, 'Dependency and self-criticism: psychological dimensions of depression', *Journal of Clinical Psychology*, 50 (1982), 113–24.
25. A. Ulanov and B. Ulanov, *Primary Speech, op. cit.*, chapter 2.
26. A. Godin, *The Psychological Dynamics of Religious Experience* (Birmingham, Ala., Religious Education Press, 1985), pp. 217–21.

## 9. Concepts of God

1. S. E. Asch, 'The metaphor: a psychological inquiry' in R. Tagiuri and L. Petrullo (eds), *Person Perception and Interpersonal Behaviour* (Stanford, Stanford University Press, 1958).

2. See also S. Ullman, 'Semantic universals' in J. H. Greenberg, *Universals of Language* (Cambridge, MIT Press, 1963).

3. J. H. M. Whiteman, *The Mystical Life* (London, Faber, 1961).

4. V. Lossky, *The Mystical Theology of the Eastern Church* (Cambridge, James Clark, 1957), p. 218.

5. *Ibid*, p. 228.

6. E. Cassirer, *Language and Myth*, trans. S. K. Langer (New York, Harper, 1946). Cassirer is a reliable guide on many issues, not just on religious cognition but in cognitive psychology generally. Indeed, the modern cognitive psychologist, Walter Weimer, has described volume three of *The Philosophy of Symbolic Forms*, published in 1929, as 'the finest cognitive psychology yet written'.

7. J. M. Soskice, *Metaphor and Religious Thought* (Oxford, Clarendon Press, 1985).

8. G. Caird, *The Language and Imagery of the Bible* (London, Duckworth, 1980).

9. O. Barfield, *Poetic Diction*, 2nd edition (London, Faber, 1952).

10. H. Werner, *Comparative Psychology of Mental Development* (Chicago, Follett Publishing Company, 1948). A similar thesis about the identity of man and nature in early language has been argued in a biblical context in N. Frye, *The Great Code: The Bible as Literature* (New York, Academic Press, 1981).

11. F. Ferré, 'Metaphor in religious discourse', in P. P. Weiner (ed), *Dictionary of the History of Ideas*, vol. 3 (New York, Charles Scribner's Sons, 1973), pp. 201–8.

12. G. Caird, *op. cit.*, p. 197.

13. W. James, *The Varieties of Religious Experience* (London, Fontana, 1960).

14. C. S. Lewis, 'Bluspels and flanasferes'. In *Rehabilitation and Other Essays* (Oxford, Oxford University Press, 1939).

15. M. Black, 'More about metaphor', in A. Ortony (ed), *Metaphor and Thought* (Cambridge, Cambridge University Press, 1979).

16. P. Edwards 'Professor Tillich's Confusions', *Mind* 74 (1965), 192–214.

17. *op. cit.*, pp. 93–6.

18. B. Goodwin, 'On morphogenic fields', *Theoria to Theory*, 13 (1979), 109–14.

19. J. Hick, 'Jesus and the world religions' in J. Hick (ed), *The Myth of God Incarnate* (London, SCM Press, 1977), p. 178.

20. R. Bultman, 'New Testament and Mythology', in H. Bartsch (ed), *Kerygma and Mythos*, trans. R. H. Fuller (New York, Harper, 1961).

21. E. Cassier, *The Philosophy of Symbolic Forms, Volume 2: Mythical Thought*, trans. R. Manheim (New Haven, Yale University Press, 1955).

22. C. G. Jung, 'The transformation symbolism of the mass', in H. Read, M. Fordham and G. Adler (eds), *The Collected Works of C. G. Jung*, vol. 11 (London, Routledge and Kegan Paul, 1958).

23. E. Cassirer, *ibid*, p. 241.

24. A. T. Welford, *Christianity: A Psychologist's Translation* (London, Hodder and Stoughton, 1971), pp. 53–4.

25. W. R. Looft and W. H. Bartz, 'Animism revisited', *Psychological Bulletin*, 71 (1969), 1–19.

26. L. B. Brown and R. H. Thouless, 'Animistic thought in civilised adults,' *Journal of Genetic Psychology*, 107 (1965), 33–42.

27. S. Erwin and G. Foster, 'The development of meaning in children's descriptive terms', *Journal of Abnormal and Social Psychology*, 61 (1960), 271–5.

28. R. W. Funk, *Language, Hermeneutic and the Word of God* (New York, Harper, 1966).

29. A. Ortony, *Metaphor and Thought* (Cambridge, Cambridge University Press, 1979).

30. R. W. Gibbs, 'Literal meaning and psychological theory', *Cognitive Science*, 8 (1984), 191–219.
31. R. R. Verbrugge, 'Resemblances in language and perception', in R. Shaw and J. Bransford (eds) *Perceiving, Acting and Knowing: Toward an Ecological Psychology* (Hillside, Lawrence Erlbaum, 1977).
32. G. Gutting, *Religious Belief and Religious Skepticism* (Notre Dame, University of Notre Dame Press, 1982).
33. St Augustine, *Confessions*, trans. R. S. Pine-Coffin (Harmondsworth, Penguin, 1961), p. 318ff.
34. See F. A. Yates, *The Art of Memory* (London, Routledge, 1966).
35. C. G. Jung, 'A psychological approach to the dogma of the Trinity', in M. Read, M. Fordham and G. Adler (eds), *The Collected Works of C. G. Jung*, vol. 11 (London, Routledge and Kegan Paul, 1958).
36. R. Panikkar, *The Trinity and the Religious Experience of Man* (London, Darton, Longman and Todd, 1973).
37. M. Masterman, 'Theism as a scientific hypothesis III, Icons: The nature of scientific revelation', *Theoria to Theory*, 1 (1967), 232–250.
38. M. Black, 'More about metaphor', in A. Ortony, *Metaphor and Thought* (Cambridge, Cambridge University Press, 1979).
39. D. Emmet, *Function, Purpose and Powers* (London, Macmillan, 1958), chapter 7.
40. J. M. Soskise, *op. cit.*, p. 158.
41. H. R. Pollio, J. M. Barlow, H. J. Fine and M. R. Pollio, *Psychology and the Poetics of Growth* (Hillsdale, Lawrence Erlbaum, 1977), chapter 6.
42. E. T. Gendlin, 'A theory of personality change', in J. T. Hart and T. M. Tomlinson (eds), *New Directions in Client-Centred Therapy* (New York, Houghton Mifflin, 1970).
43. L. N. Rice and A. K. Wagstaff, 'Client voice quality and expressive style as indices of productive psychotherapy', *Journal of Consulting Psychology*, 31 (1967), 557–63.
44. N. J. Esposito and L. H. Pelton 'Review of the measurement of semantic satiation', *Psychological Bulletin*, 75 (1971), 330–46.
45. H. J. Werner and B. Kaplan, *Symbol Formation* (London, John Wiley, 1963).
46. F. I. M. Craik and R. S. Lockhart, 'Levels of processing, a framework for memory research', *Journal of Verbal Learning and Verbal Behaviour*, 11 (1972), 671–84.
47. Ignatius Loyola, *Spiritual Exercises*, trans. T. Corbishley (London, A. Clark, 1973), see especially the 'second method of prayer'.

# Index